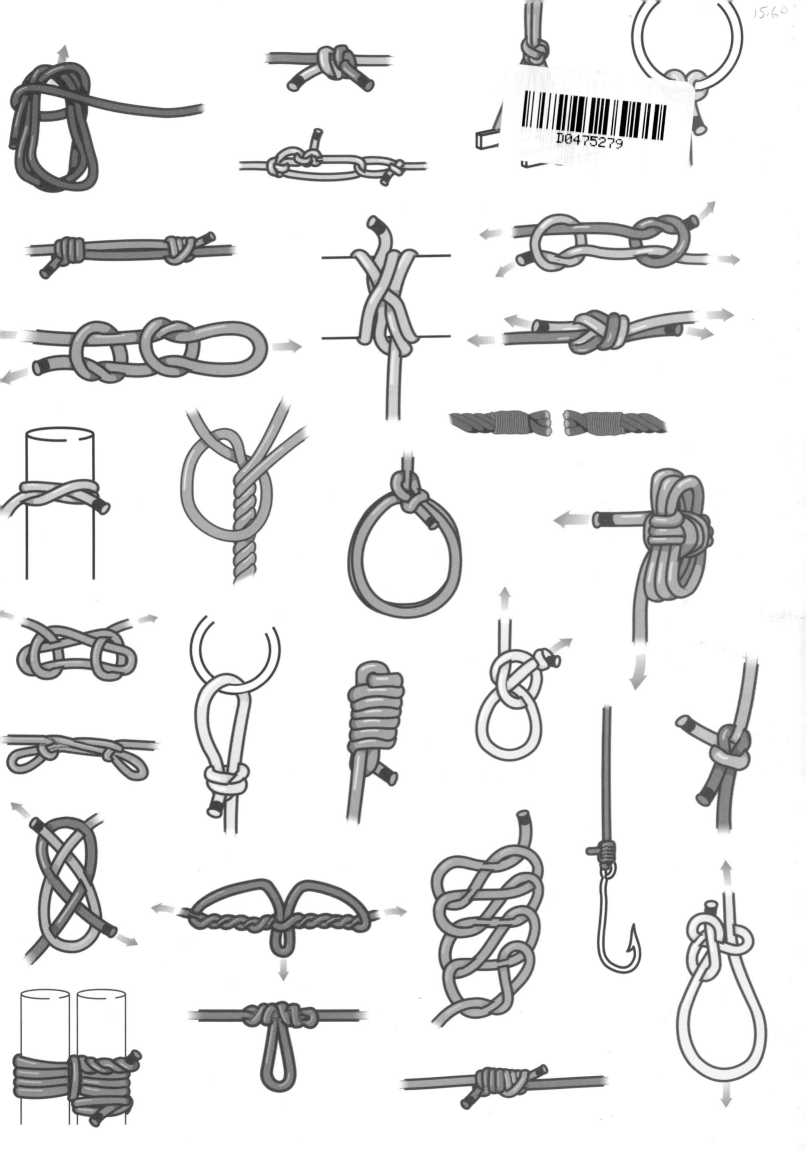

15.60

KNOTS

A Step-by-Step Guide to Tying Loops, Hitches, Bends, and Dozens of Other Useful Knots

By Kenneth S. Burton, Jr.

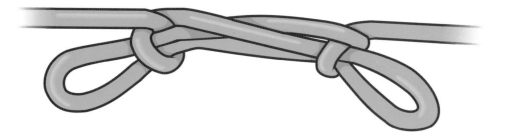

Illustrated by Robert Frawley

COURAGE
B O O K S

AN IMPRINT OF RUNNING PRESS
PHILADELPHIA • LONDON

Library of Congress Cataloging-in-Publication
Number 96-69267

ISBN 0-7624-0067-6

Book cover package designed by Diane Miljat
Book interior designed by Stan Green
Edited by Mary McGuire

Published by Courage Books, an imprint of
Running Press Book Publishers
125 South Twenty-second Street
Philadelphia, Pennsylvania 19103-4399

For my best girl:
Sarah Marie Burton

Contents

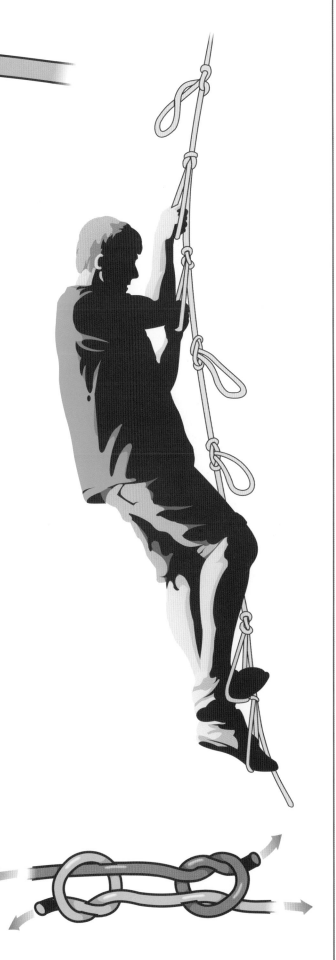

Introduction

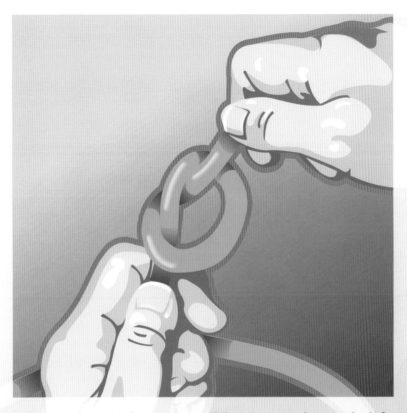

Only in recent years has it been possible to go through life without a solid working knowledge of knots. In the past, almost every occupation had specific knots associated with it, and newcomers to a job were quite literally "shown the ropes." While a deep understanding of rope and knots is seldom required on the job these days, you only need to visit the parking lot of your local home center on any weekend to see why everyone should know at least a handful of basic knots (it's surprising that there aren't more car accidents involving plywood that wasn't adequately secured to the tops of automobiles).

The knots selected for this book are some of the more useful, general purpose ones. They've been divided into chapters based on their uses. Learning one or two knots from each chapter should provide you with a solution for most knot-related problems. As with any skill, you'll do better if you practice tying these knots occasionally. A length or two of ¼-inch or ⁵⁄₁₆-inch diameter line will prove handy for this purpose.

One cautionary note: This book will provide an excellent starting point for learning about knots, but before trusting your life to any of the knots shown here (as you might do when rock climbing), find someone knowledgeable to check what you've learned.

Choosing the Right Rope

When you set out to buy a rope, you'll likely face a bewildering array of choices. Your local home center should stock over a dozen kinds of rope in many different diameters. Unfortunately, few sales people at such centers are very knowledgable about rope, and rope manufacturers tend to provide more information on what you should NOT do with the rope rather than on what you should or can do with it. Two figures the manufacturers will tell you, however, are the breaking strength and the safe working load (SWL). These numbers are usually listed in pounds and will give you an idea of how strong the rope is. The SWL will be lower than the breaking strength and is the number you should pay the most attention to.

So, if you're looking for a rope for a certain use, say rock climbing or logging, you're probably better off shopping in a place that stocks that kind of specialized equipment. The sales people at such a store should be able to help you choose exactly what you need, though it may end up costing a bit more.

But for many everyday applications, such as running guy lines for a dining fly, hanging a rope swing, or tying down a tarp, you won't require any special type of rope. For these purposes, almost any of the available ropes will do. What you want to look for is a rope of the appropriate diameter (which will determine its strength) that can be tied easily with the types of knots you're likely to be

using. The best way to figure these things out is to try to tie some knots in the rope before you buy it.

In general, you want a fairly flexible rope that holds knots well. Knots will be difficult to draw up snugly in a rope that's too stiff, and they may slip. But a rope that's too limp may stretch more that you can safely tolerate.

You'll find that ropes vary in both the way they are made, and in the material they are made from. In general, ropes are either "laid up" (twisted from three strands), or they are braided (plaited) from more strands. Three strand, or "hawser laid" rope is traditional, while braided line is a more recent invention. In general, braided lines are smoother and more supple than laid up ropes, making them easier to tie, but they also tend to be more slippery, so your knots may tend to slip.

You can still buy rope made from manila and other natural fibers, although synthetic materials are becoming more and more common. The one place where manila rope has a real edge is where a rope will be subject to high heat. Synthetic ropes will melt if they're exposed to enough heat. The most common ropes available are made from one (or more) of these four synthetic materials:

Nylon

There are two types of nylon rope available. The better, stronger type is made from continuous filament nylon; the individual fibers that make up the rope strands are quite long. Spun nylon is made of shorter fibers. It has a fuzzier appearance, and is softer to the touch.

Nylon rope is quite strong and elastic. It is heavier than water, so it will sink, making them inappropriate for rescue lines. It absorbs sudden loads well by stretching, not unlike a big rubber band. Because of this combination of strength and elasticity, nylon rope is a great choice for tow lines and mooring ropes.

Polyester

Polyester rope is more commonly known by its tradename DACRON. While it's almost as strong as nylon, it lacks nylon's elasticity and ability to

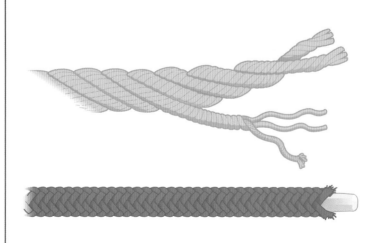

absorb shock. But, whereas nylon can lose up to ten percent of its strength when wet, polyester retains almost its full strength and durability even when soaked.

Polyester rope is an excellent choice for lines that need to stay under tension without stretching—guy lines for transplanted trees and sail halliards fall into this category. It also makes good, general-purpose rope.

Polypropylene and Polyethylene

These two cheaper synthetics have very similar characteristics. However, polypropylene has a slight performance edge. Both are light in weight and float—an important characteristic for rescue or water-ski tow lines.

Both filaments also have a fairly low melting point—low enough that the friction from one rope sliding past another can generate enough heat to melt and separate one or the other lines. Both are about half the strength of nylon, (but twice as strong as manila). And both are sensitive to ultraviolet light, so they should be stored out of sunlight if possible. Generally, polypropylene and polyethylene ropes are not as good as those made of nylon or polyester, although the two fibers often are intermingled with those of the more expensive synthetics to yield rope of good quality.

Caring for Rope

A good quality rope will last a long time if it's taken care of properly. For example, it should be inspected from time to time for cuts, worn areas, and discoloration, which may indicate chemical deterioration. While synthetic ropes won't rot like those made from natural fibers, they're still susceptible to deterioration. This might occur from sun exposure, or contact with chemicals.

A rope should also be protected from dirt and abrasion. Obviously, too much abrasion can cause a rope to wear quickly. But dirt can contribute to this by becoming embedded in the rope fibers and slowly wearing them away from within. Try to avoid dragging or pulling ropes over jagged surfaces and edges. Also try to keep your ropes off the ground as much as possible. A dirty rope should be washed with gentle detergent and rinsed clean—especially if it's been exposed to salt water. A rope that isn't rinsed of salt water will never truly dry because the residual salt embedded in the fibers will continually absorb moisture from the air. After cleaning, dry the rope thoroughly (do this even with synthetic ones) before coiling them for storage. (See pages 14–15 for details on coiling.)

Surprisingly, one of the most harmful things you can do to a rope is to tie a knot in it. As useful as they are, knots stress ropes by kinking the fibers, thereby weakening them. In fact, some knots can weaken the breaking strength of a rope by as much as fifty percent. To avoid damaging your ropes, learn to tie the right knots for the job at hand, and try to use knots that cause the least amount of stress to a rope. Finally, when you are finished with a rope, always completely untie it to allow the fibers to relax.

Chapter 1
Rope Basics

Skill with rope not only lies with tying the appropriate knot for the job and the rope you're using, but in how you handle and treat the rope itself. A properly coiled rope is ready to use almost instantly, all that is usually required is a simple shake to free the loops. Ropes that are improperly stored and cared for won't last very long and won't be ready for use when you need them most.

Whipping Rope Ends

One of the best things you can do to take care a rope it to "whip" its ends. Whipping refers to the process of wrapping the ends of a rope with "small stuff"—finer cord, such as dental floss or string. This preparation is especially important with natural-fiber ropes because it keeps the ends from unraveling. Synthetic ropes don't suffer as much from this problem because they are generally melted at the ends to fuse the fibers together. However a synthetic rope will still benefit from being whipped.

Whipping makes the end of a rope a little bit stiffer than the unwhipped part. Thus a whipped end functions like a needle as you tie knots; you can poke it through tight loops and in between turns with ease. Make your whippings slightly longer than the diameter of the rope.

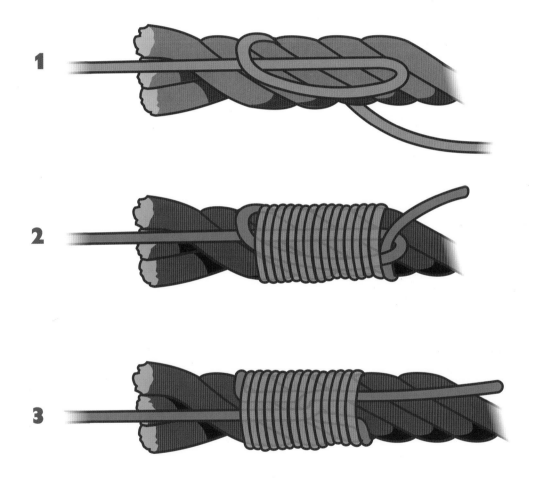

CUTTING A ROPE

Before you cut a rope, whip it on either side of the intended cut, leaving a space in between about ¼- to ½-inch long. Cut the rope in the middle of this space. If you are using synthetic rope, melt the ends back almost to the whipping with a match or cigarette lighter. Take care not to set the rope on fire.

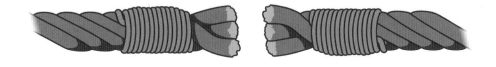

The Basic Coil

A rope's basic "instinct" is to become a hopeless tangle. You're most likely to discover this some rainy night, while trying to set up a tent. Fortunately, you can prevent such problems by simply coiling your ropes before storing them. The basic coil is most useful for ropes 20 feet and longer. Each loop in the coil should take up 3 to 4 feet of rope.

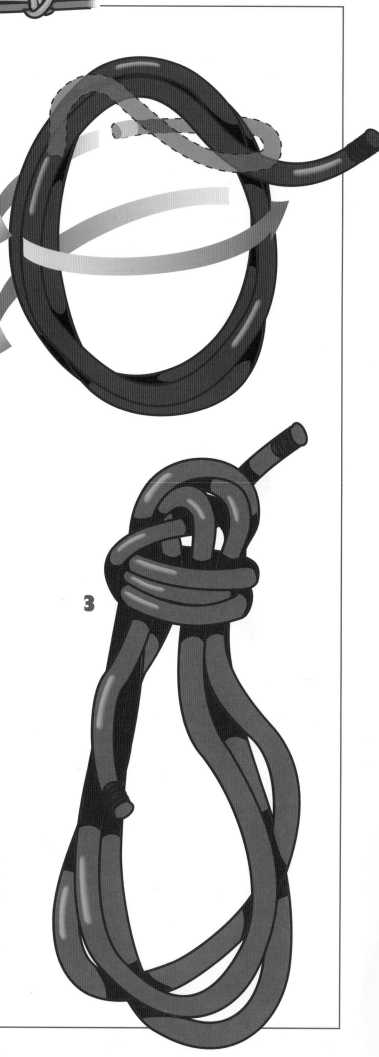

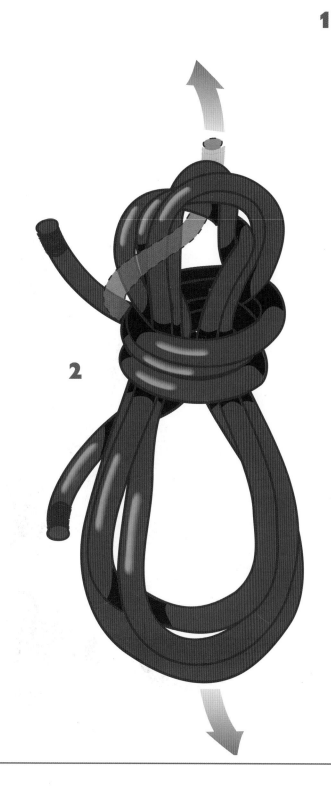

The Overhand Coil

The Overhand Coil is useful for pieces of rope that are not more that 20 feet long. It's essentially a loose Overhand Knot tied with the coil itself. Once you acquire the knack, it's very easy to tie. Untying it is simple too, provided you pull on the right parts. If you don't, the rope may become snarled.

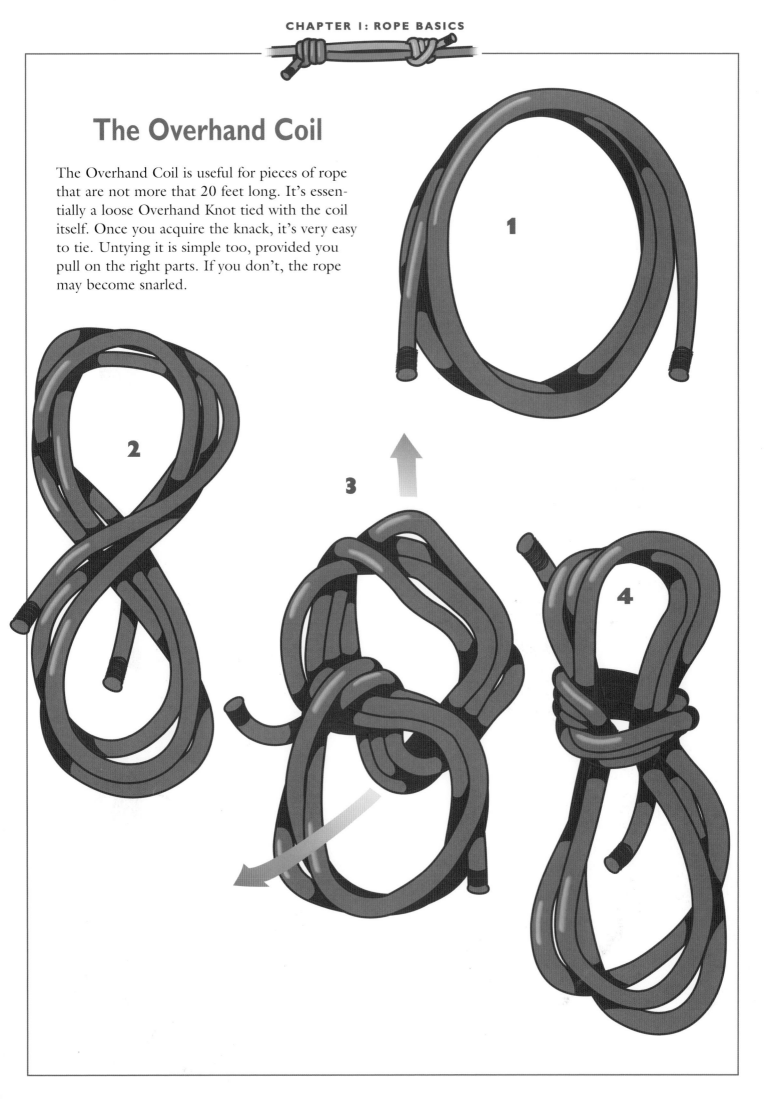

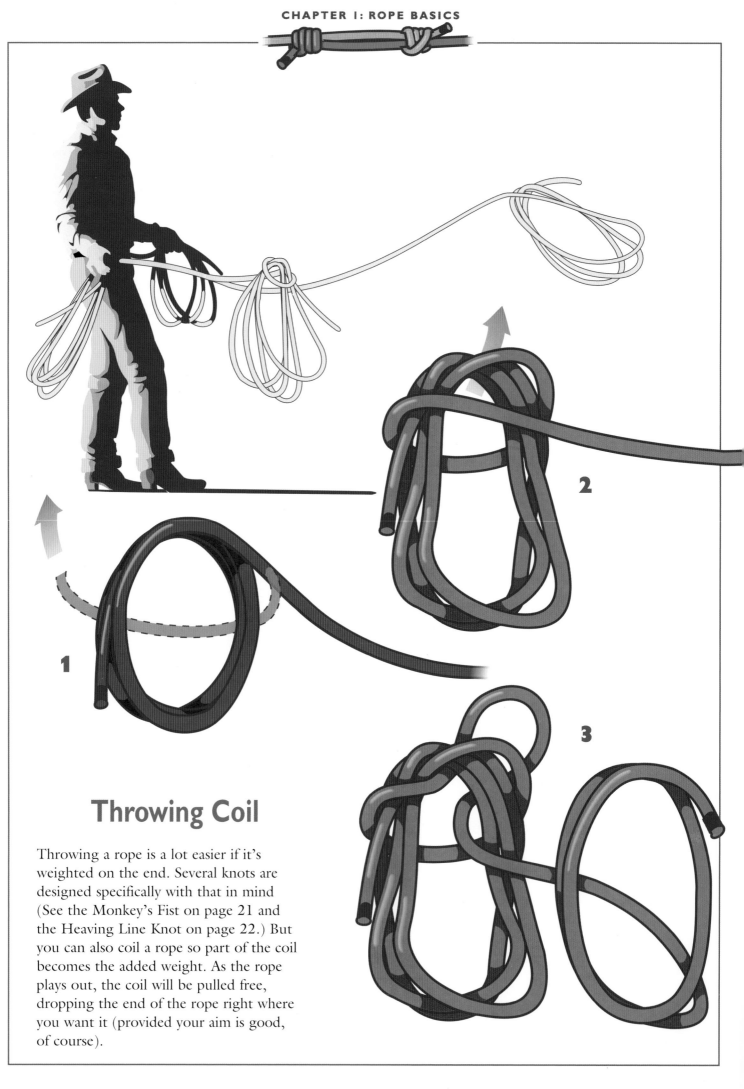

1

2

3

Throwing Coil

Throwing a rope is a lot easier if it's weighted on the end. Several knots are designed specifically with that in mind (See the Monkey's Fist on page 21 and the Heaving Line Knot on page 22.) But you can also coil a rope so part of the coil becomes the added weight. As the rope plays out, the coil will be pulled free, dropping the end of the rope right where you want it (provided your aim is good, of course).

Chapter 2

End and Stopper Knots

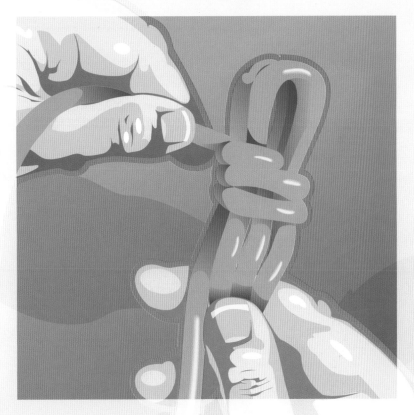

Stopper knots are generally tied at the end of a rope to keep the rope from pulling through an eye, a hole (like a grommet), or even part of another knot. They are also used occasionally to keep the end of a rope from unraveling, although this practice has some drawbacks. Having a clunky knot at the end of a rope can make it difficult pass the end through the various loops required to tie other knots; and some stopper knots can actually damage the rope fibers.

Stopper knots range in complexity. The Overhand Loop knot (page 20) is as simple a knot as there is, while the Monkey's Fist (page 21) is much more elaborate. Typically, sailors would tie large, fancy stopper knots to decorate shipboard items such a bell pulls and sea chest handles.

The Overhand Knot

Also known as the Single or Thumb Knot

This is the smallest and simplest of all knots and it serves as the base for many complex knots. It's often tied at the end of a length of rope to keep the rope from slipping through an eye, or grommet. As simple as it is, the overhand knot is not a very good knot. It can be difficult to untie and can damage the rope fibers. In general, it's best to limit its use to twine, thread and other small stuff.

The Figure Eight Knot

Also known as the Flemish Knot

The Figure Eight knot is your best choice for a general-purpose stopper knot. It's larger and much stronger than the Overhand knot. It also remains easy to untie, even when pulled tight, and it doesn't injure the rope's fibers.

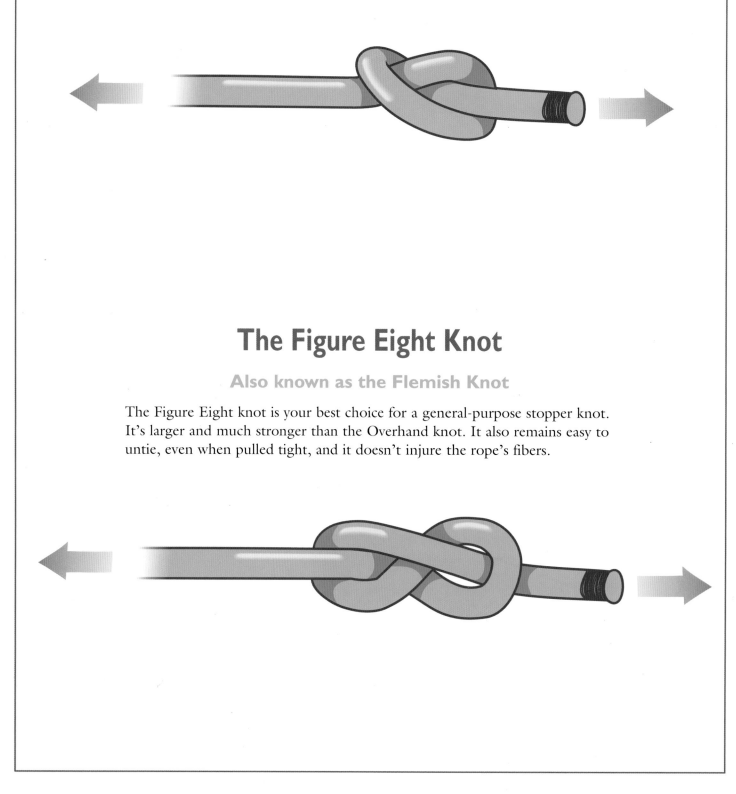

The Stevedore's Knot

Even bulkier than the Figure Eight Knot, the Stevedore's Knot is good for keeping a knot from pulling through a large eye. It's commonly used on ropes running through a ship's cargo blocks (pulleys), which have fairly large openings where the rope passes through. An extra turn make the knot even larger, as shown.

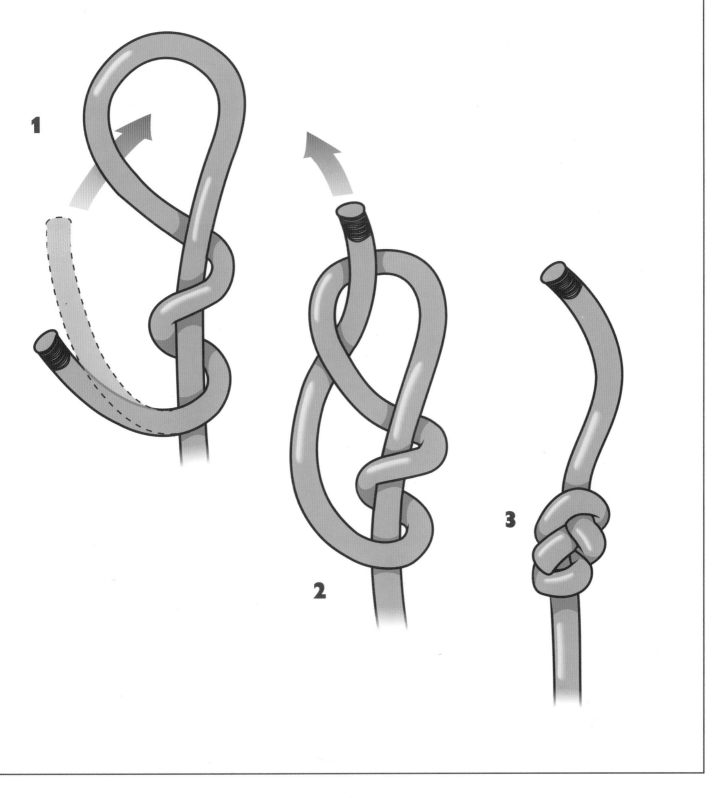

19

The Overhand Loop

You can tie a quick but bulky stopper knot by making an Overhand Knot in the midsection (bight) of a rope. This is handy when you need a stopper knot along the rope's length and don't have ready access to its ends. (Also see the Figure Eight Loop on page 50.) You can also use this knot to isolate part of a rope that's worn or damaged. Keep in mind it's difficult to untie and can damage the rope fibers, especially if pulled extremely tight.

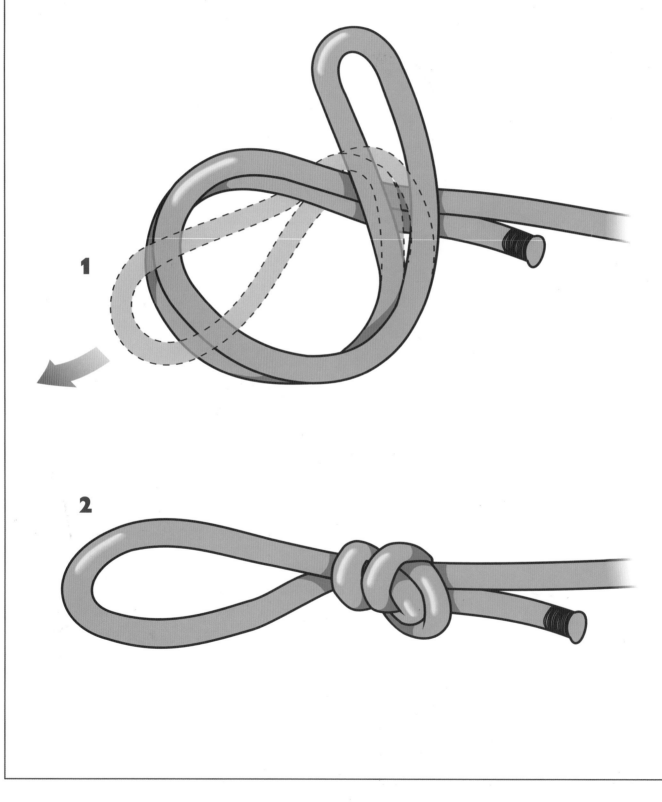

The Monkey's Fist

The Monkey's Fist is a decorative way to add weight to the end of a rope to make the rope easier to throw. By itself, the knot probably won't be heavy enough to make that much difference in how far the rope carries. But if you insert a small round stone in the center, before working the knot tight, the knot will have an adequate heft to it.

The Heaving Line Knot

This knot is another way to add weight to the end of a line to make it carry farther when you throw it. While not as classy as the Monkey's Fist, the Heaving Line Knot is much faster to tie—an advantage if you don't have a rope you can dedicate to throwing. Tied in ¾-inch diameter (or heavier) rope, this knot also makes a first-class fender you can throw over the side of a boat to protect the boat from damage.

1

2

3

Matthew Walker's Knot

While laid-up ropes are slowly losing ground to braided ones, it still pays to know at least one stopper knot that is tied directly in the strands of the rope itself. The Matthew Walker Knot is one of the finest. It's good-looking, quite strong, and fiendishly difficult to un-tie. After you tie the knot, twist the strands back together and whip the end of the rope to finish.

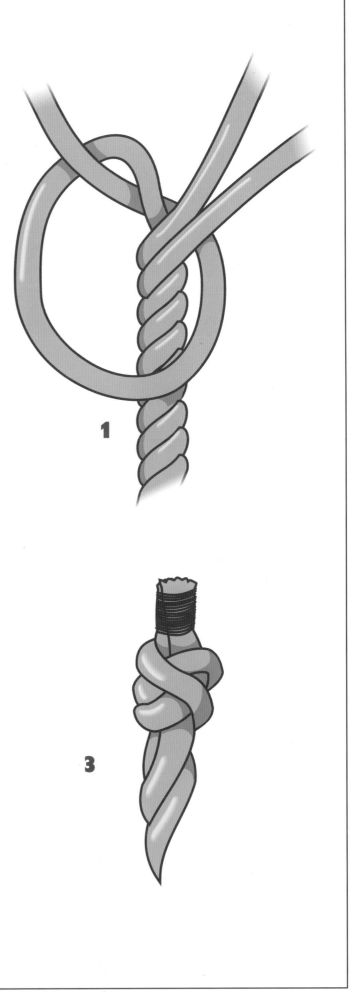

23

Chapter 3
Hitches

Hitches are among the most common and most useful knots because they are used to tie ropes onto other objects such as poles, rings, and stakes. When deciding which hitch to tie, you have to take into consideration the load that will be placed on the line (heavy or light; shifting or stationary) as well as how long the rope will hold the load (5 minutes or overnight). The easily tied hitches may not hold as securely as the more difficult ones, but may be a better choice if you need to undo them often or quickly.

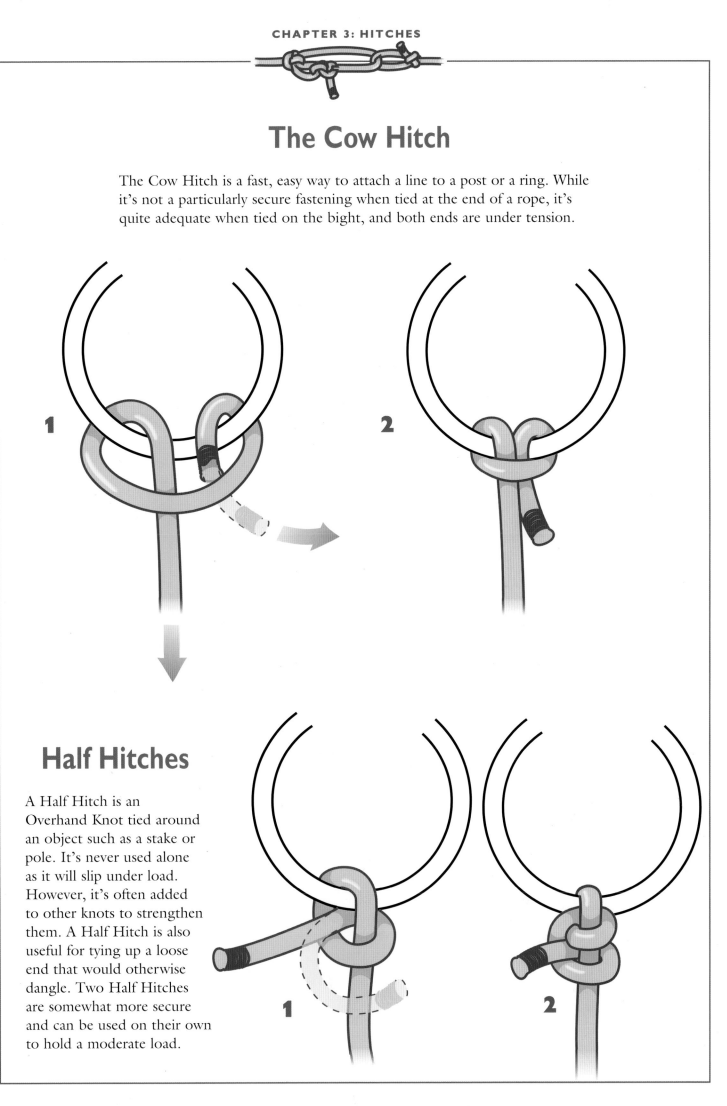

The Cow Hitch

The Cow Hitch is a fast, easy way to attach a line to a post or a ring. While it's not a particularly secure fastening when tied at the end of a rope, it's quite adequate when tied on the bight, and both ends are under tension.

1

2

Half Hitches

A Half Hitch is an Overhand Knot tied around an object such as a stake or pole. It's never used alone as it will slip under load. However, it's often added to other knots to strengthen them. A Half Hitch is also useful for tying up a loose end that would otherwise dangle. Two Half Hitches are somewhat more secure and can be used on their own to hold a moderate load.

1

2

The Tautline Hitch

Also known as the Midshipman's Hitch

This hitch is very useful for rigging tents and tarps because it can slide along the standing part of the rope to take up slack. If tied tightly, the knot will hold its position, keeping the rope taut.

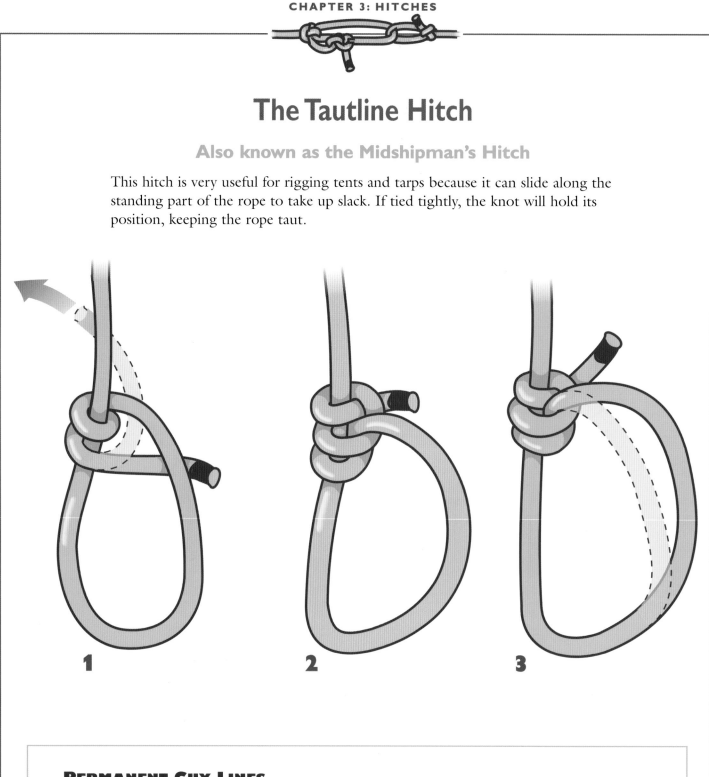

1   **2**   **3**

PERMANENT GUY LINES

Guy Lines are ropes that run from the top of the pole to a stake in the ground. When properly tensioned, Guy Lines help to keep the pole upright. If you have a number of ropes you use only for rigging a tent, you can easily make up a set of dedicated, adjustable Guy Lines to save you the bother of having to tie a lot of knots each time you set up. Drill holes in both ends of a short length of wood. (Use a hard wood such as oak, and make the pieces approximately $3/8$-inch thick x $3/4$-inch wide x 3-inch long.) The diameter of the holes should match that of your rope. Sand the pieces to ease the sharp corners. Then pass the end of the ropes through the holes and tie off the end with a stopper knot as shown. The wooden toggles will allow you to adjust the tension on your lines and will hold fast even in a summer squall.

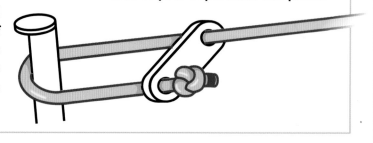

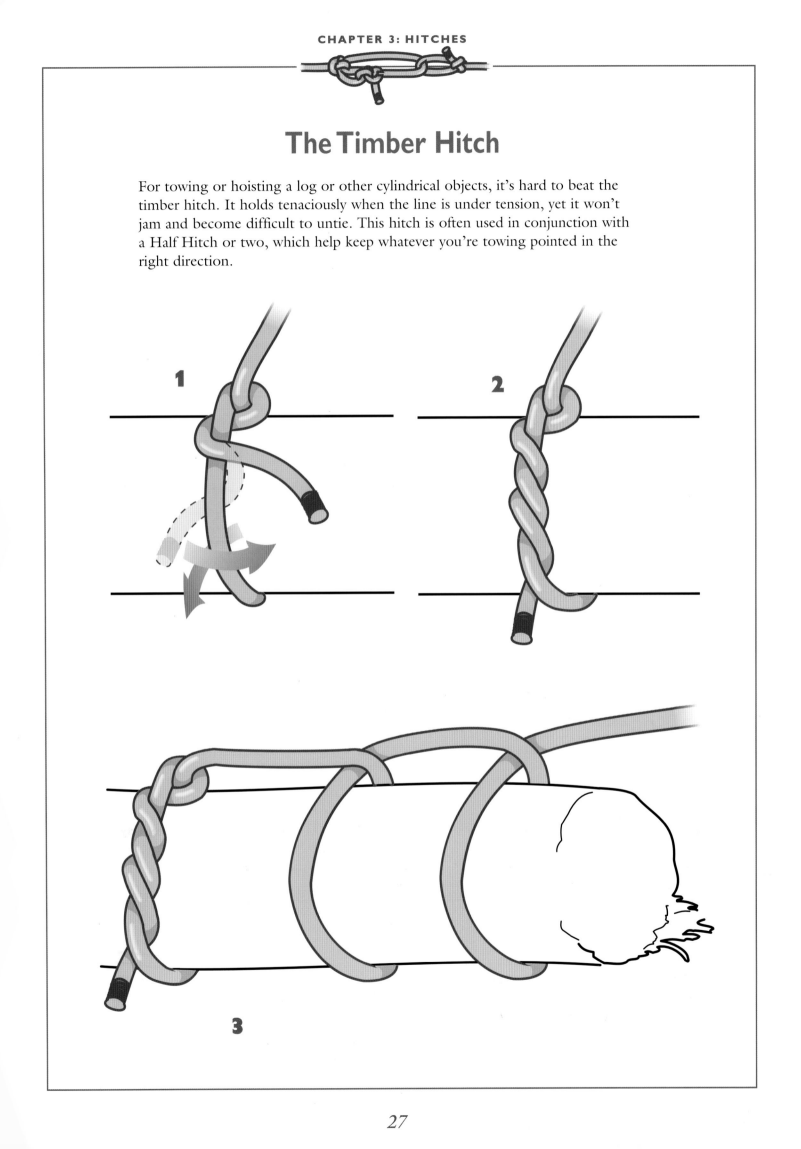

The Timber Hitch

For towing or hoisting a log or other cylindrical objects, it's hard to beat the timber hitch. It holds tenaciously when the line is under tension, yet it won't jam and become difficult to untie. This hitch is often used in conjunction with a Half Hitch or two, which help keep whatever you're towing pointed in the right direction.

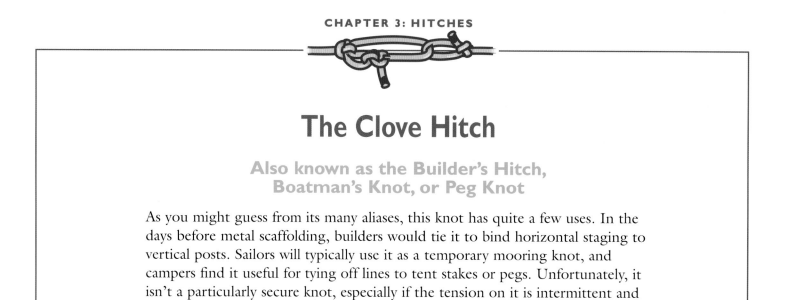

The Clove Hitch

Also known as the Builder's Hitch, Boatman's Knot, or Peg Knot

As you might guess from its many aliases, this knot has quite a few uses. In the days before metal scaffolding, builders would tie it to bind horizontal staging to vertical posts. Sailors will typically use it as a temporary mooring knot, and campers find it useful for tying off lines to tent stakes or pegs. Unfortunately, it isn't a particularly secure knot, especially if the tension on it is intermittent and shifts position, as it might with a moored boat. Always consider this knot a temporary solution.

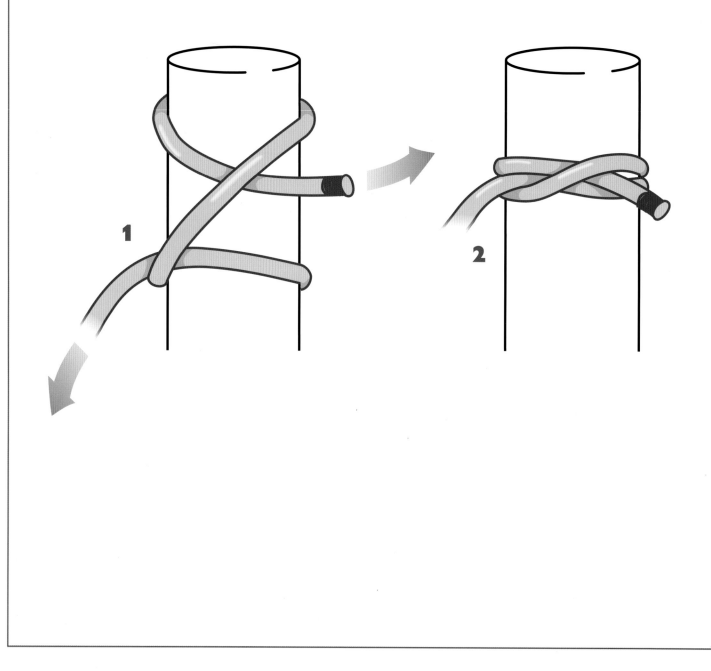

The Mooring Hitch

A variation of the Clove Hitch (page 28), the Mooring Hitch is a more secure means of fastening a line to a pole. You do, however, need to have access to the pole's end.

In order to tie the knot you have to be able to throw a loop over it.

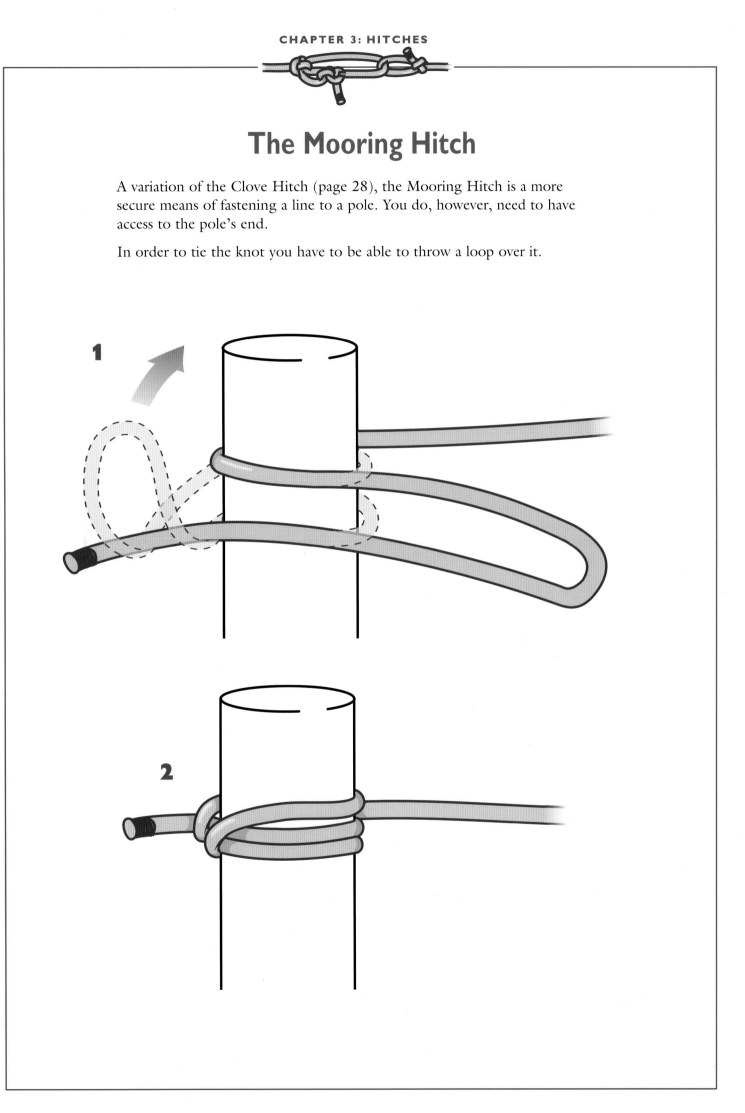

The Neck Halter

As its name implies, this knot is used for tethering an animal. It's really a combination of two simple knots, the Figure Eight and the Overhand. Tie a loose Figure Eight Knot in the bight (center) of the rope, leaving enough of the working end to loop around the animal's neck. Tie an overhand knot at the end of the rope and tuck it through the Figure Eight. Then pull the Figure Eight Knot tight. The Neck Halter won't choke the animal because it doesn't slip. But DON'T confuse this knot with the Halter Hitch (page 54), which will tighten around an animal's neck.

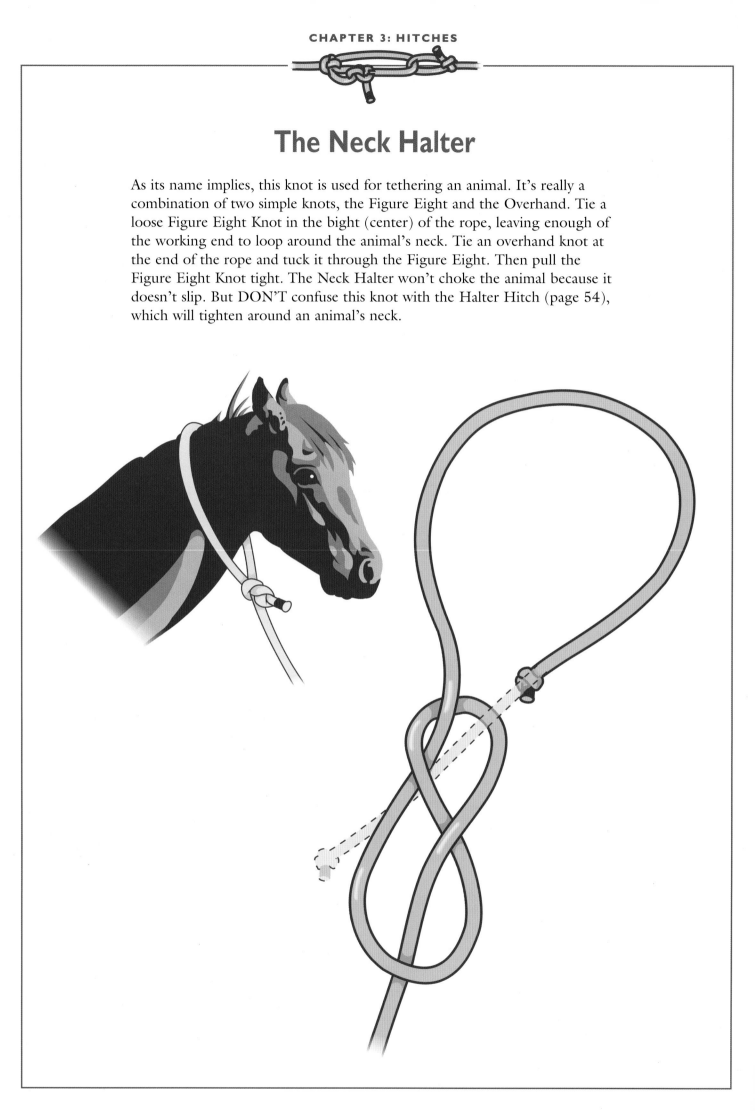

The Trucker's Hitch

Here's another hitch that is actually a combination of several other knots. It starts with a Bowline (page 43) on one end combined with a Figure Eight Loop (page 50) and two Half-Hitches on the other.

This knot is especially useful for tying cargo to the bed of a trailer, or to a car's roof rack because it allows you to cinch down the load and keep tension on the rope as you finish tying. It's worth learning just so you can feel smug in the home center parking lot, easily—and securely—tying plywood onto your car.

The Halliard Hitch

The Halliard Hitch is another secure way to attach a line to a pole or post. When it's all drawn up, it presents a very neat appearance. This combination of aesthetics and security makes the knot an excellent choice for such tasks as stringing a rope from stanchion to stanchion for crowd control.

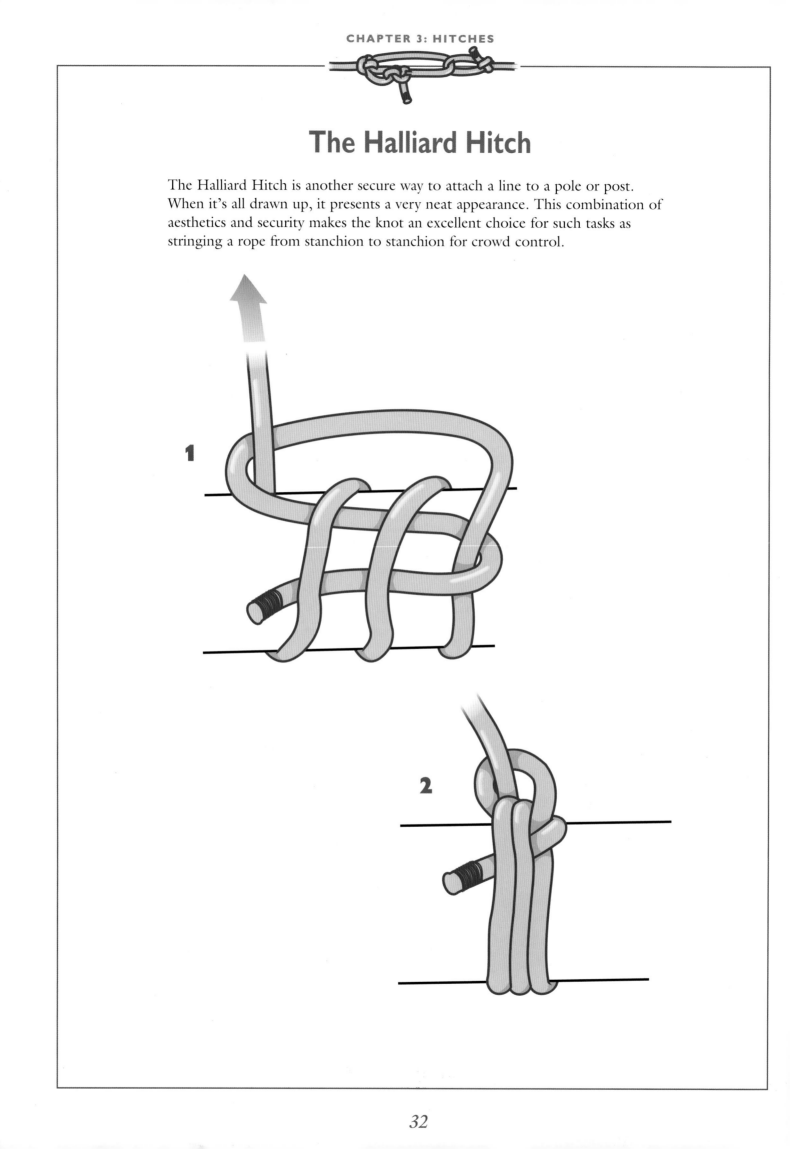

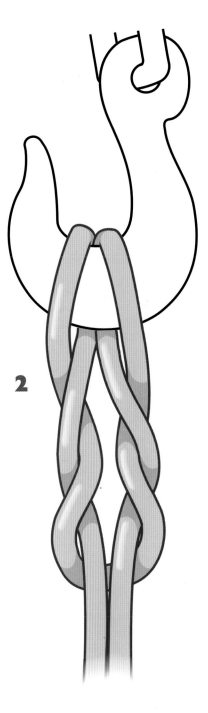

1

2

The Catspaw Hitch

Also known as the Hook Hitch

The Catspaw Hitch is used almost exclusively to attach a line to a hook for hoisting or towing. For light loads, it can be tied at the end of a rope. But for heavy lifting, it should be tied in the middle, leaving both ends free to carry the load. This knot won't jam, and it comes untied instantly when removed from the hook.

The Fisherman's Bend

Also known as the Anchor Bend

Despite being termed a bend (which usually suggests that it's used to join two ropes together), this knot is one of the most reliable ways to tie a rope to a pole or other object. The extra turn helps distribute the load, keeping the knot from jamming and becoming difficult to untie.

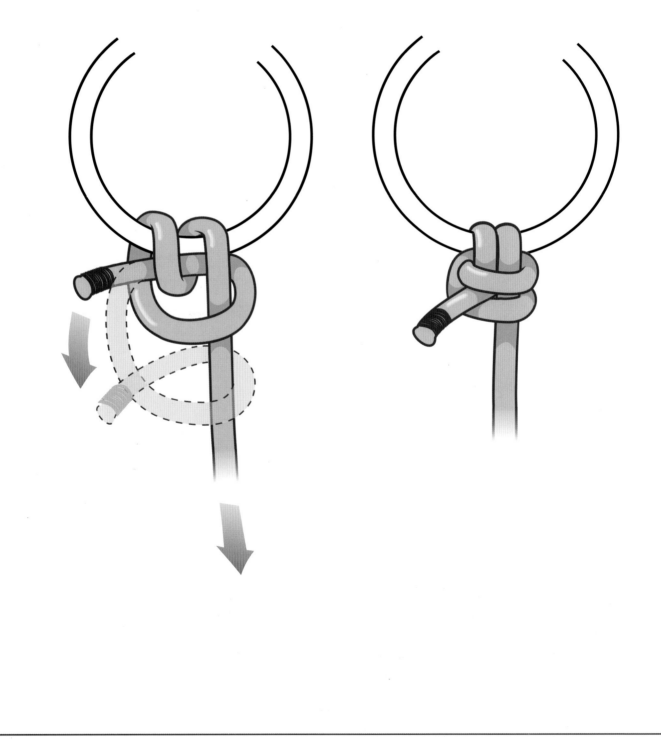

The Swing Hitch

Like the Mooring Hitch, this knot is a variation of the Clove Hitch. But unlike the Clove Hitch, the Swing Hitch is very secure. Even when subjected to a shifting load, the Swing Hitch maintains its grip on whatever it's tied around. This makes it a prime candidate for hanging a rope swing because it won't slip and chafe the branch it's tied around or wear itself in two.

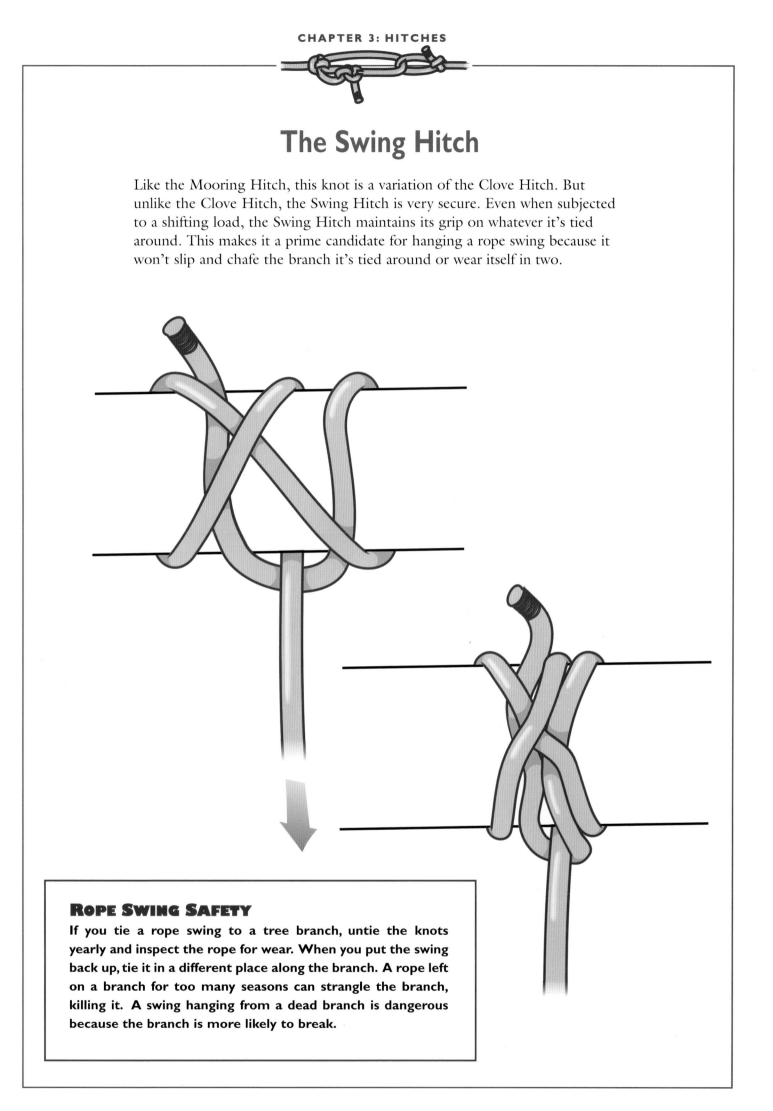

ROPE SWING SAFETY

If you tie a rope swing to a tree branch, untie the knots yearly and inspect the rope for wear. When you put the swing back up, tie it in a different place along the branch. A rope left on a branch for too many seasons can strangle the branch, killing it. A swing hanging from a dead branch is dangerous because the branch is more likely to break.

The Sliding Ring Hitch

Also known as the Italian Hitch and the Munter Friction Hitch

Unlike most of the other hitches, this knot isn't supposed to hold fast. Rather, it's supposed to slide freely through a carabiner when the line is slack, but jam up tight under tension. It's used extensively by climbers when belaying (securing) each other for safety. Before you put this knot to the test on a rock face, have a qualified person check out your mastery of it. For being such a simple knot, it's all too easy to tie wrong.

1

2

Chapter 4

Binding Knots

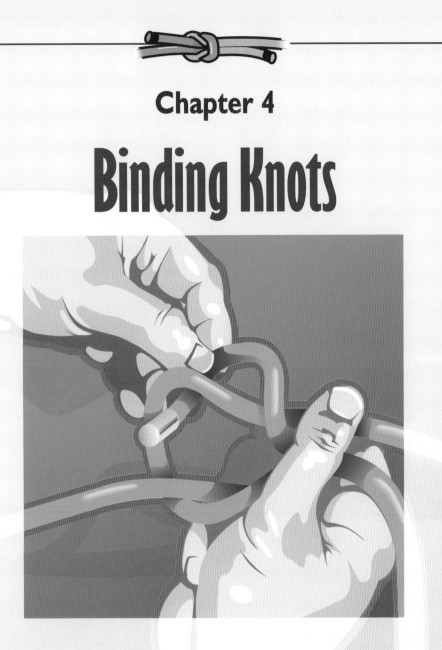

Binding knots are meant to tie objects together or closed, such as bags and packages. In fact, one of the first knots you probably learned how to tie was a Binding Knot—in your shoe laces. The most familiar is the Square (or Reef) Knot. This is the knot your grandmother had you put a finger on as she tied up a package for shipping. It's still a much-used knot, although there are a handful of others that also worth learning.

The Square Knot

Also known as the Reef Knot

This knot's alias belies its nautical background. It's commonly used aboard ships to reef, or shorten the sails in a strong wind. It can be readily untied, which makes it ideal for this purpose because sailors have to react quickly to changing situations. It has many other uses for dry land, as well—binding packages, tying shoelaces (with bows, of course), and cinching bags closed. Because the Square Knot is one of the few knots many people know, you will often see it used to tie two pieces of rope together. This, however, can even be dangerous if the ropes are subjected to a heavy load, because the Square Knot will slip or "capsize" readily under tension.

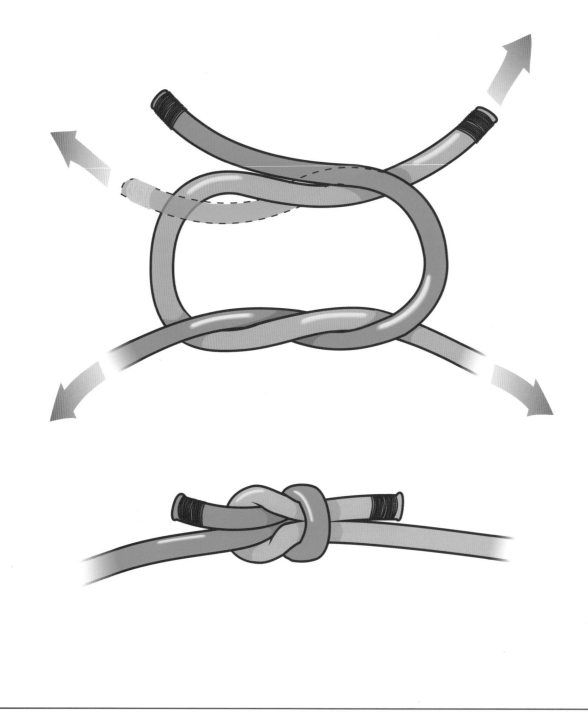

The Thief Knot and The Granny Knot

These two binding knots are poor relations to the Square Knot. Both hold poorly and will slip completely under load. The only reason they are worth knowing about is to prevent your tying one by mistake. The Thief Knot is particularly insidious because it so closely resembles the true Square Knot. According to legend, sailors would tie their seabags closed with a Thief Knot, assuming that a thief would probably retie the bag with a Square Knot. This would alert the bag's owner that his bag had been violated, however so would the fact that there were things missing from inside, so it isn't clear exactly what a sailor would gain from this little bit of intrigue.

The Granny Knot

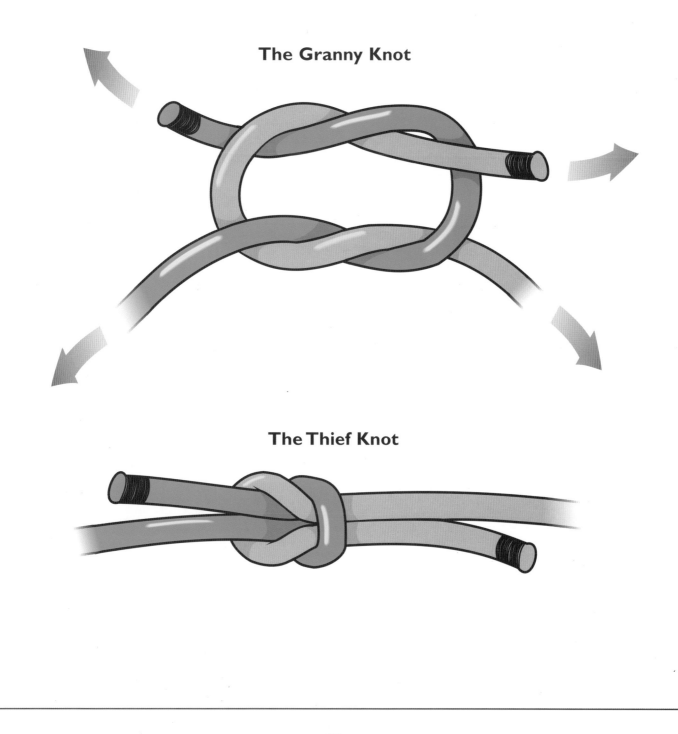

The Thief Knot

The Surgeon's Knot

This knot is favored by surgeon's because the first turns stay tight while the second stage of the knot is tied. This is quite useful for tying off blood vessels. Outside of the operating room, it's usually tied in twine or string. In heavier line, this knot is somewhat ungainly because of its asymmetrical construction and may require a little coaxing to draw up well.

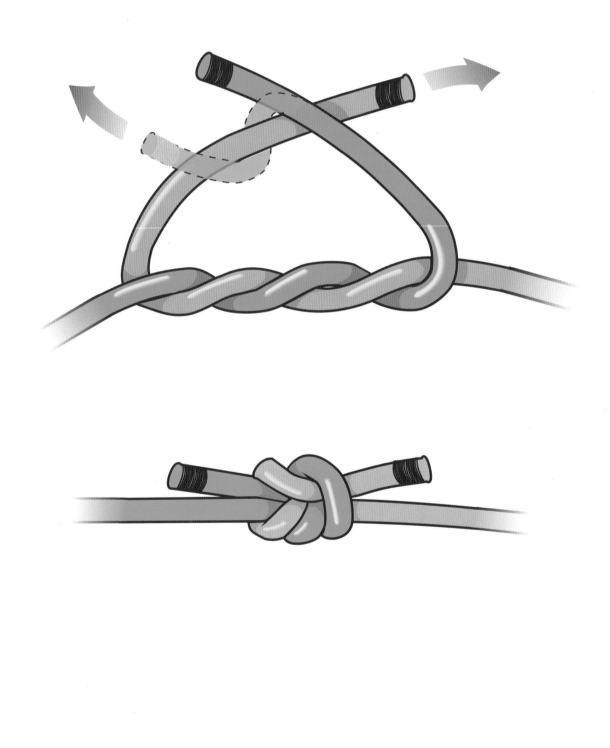

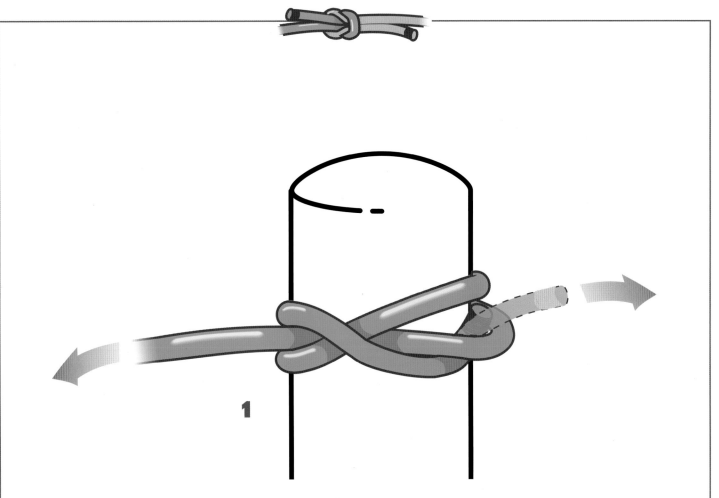

1

The Constrictor Knot

Of the binding knots presented here, the Constrictor Knot is the strongest and most secure. It draws up well and won't slip. If you look at the knot closely, you'll see that it's a variation of the Clove Hitch (page 28), with the working end tucked through one of the turns. This added tuck is what gives the knot is strength. In addition to its use as a binding knot, for tying up bags and so forth, it also makes a secure hitch for attaching a line to a post or pole.

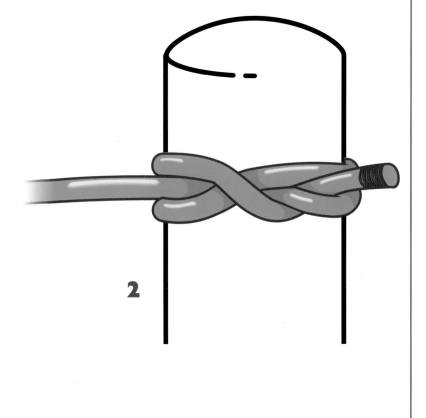

2

Chapter 5
Loop Knots

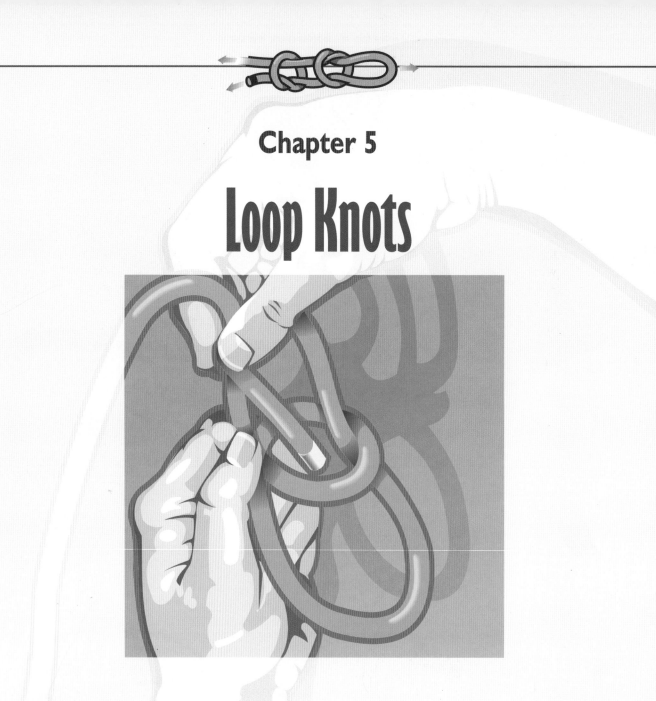

Like hitches, loops can be used to attach ropes to other objects. But instead of being tied directly to the object and cinched up tight as a hitch is, a loop is usually tied separately and dropped over the object afterwards. This generally means a loop can be removed from an object without being untied—a handy feature when a rope is repeatedly used for the same purpose.

The Bowline

Also known as The Bulin

If you only learn one loop knot, the Bowline is one to learn because it has so many uses. It's very strong and won't slip readily, nor will it jam, making difficult to untie. (Although you should be sure to draw it up snugly, especially when it's tied in stiff, synthetic rope.) It's a fun knot to teach to young children, because you can tell a "story" as you perform the steps necessary to tie it: The rabbit (the end of the rope, figure 1) comes out of his hole, goes around the tree (figure 2), and dives back into his hole (figure 3). For a more convincing "rabbit," try tying a small, Spanish Bowline (page 46) in the end of the line before starting the story.

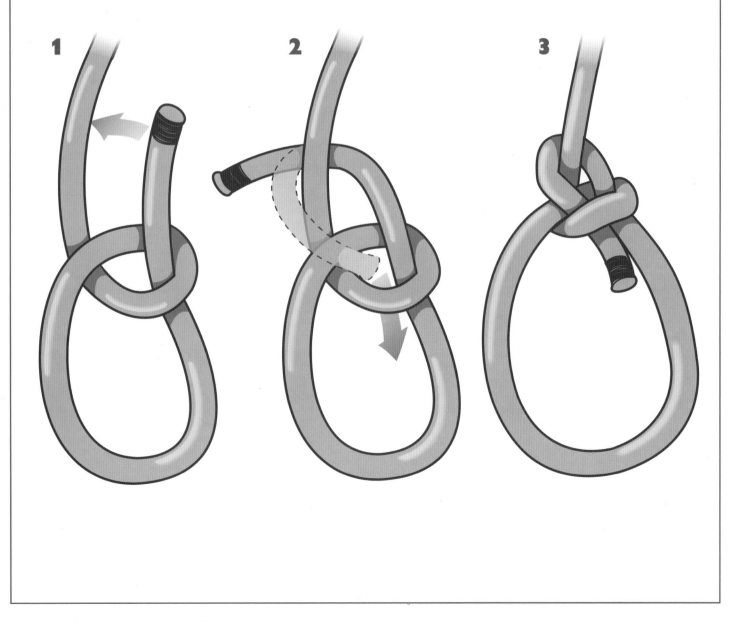

The Bowline on the Bight

The bight of a rope is the part of the rope that's between the two ends. This knot makes two strong, fixed loops in the middle of a rope. It's especially handy when you don't have access to the end of the rope to tie a regular bowline.

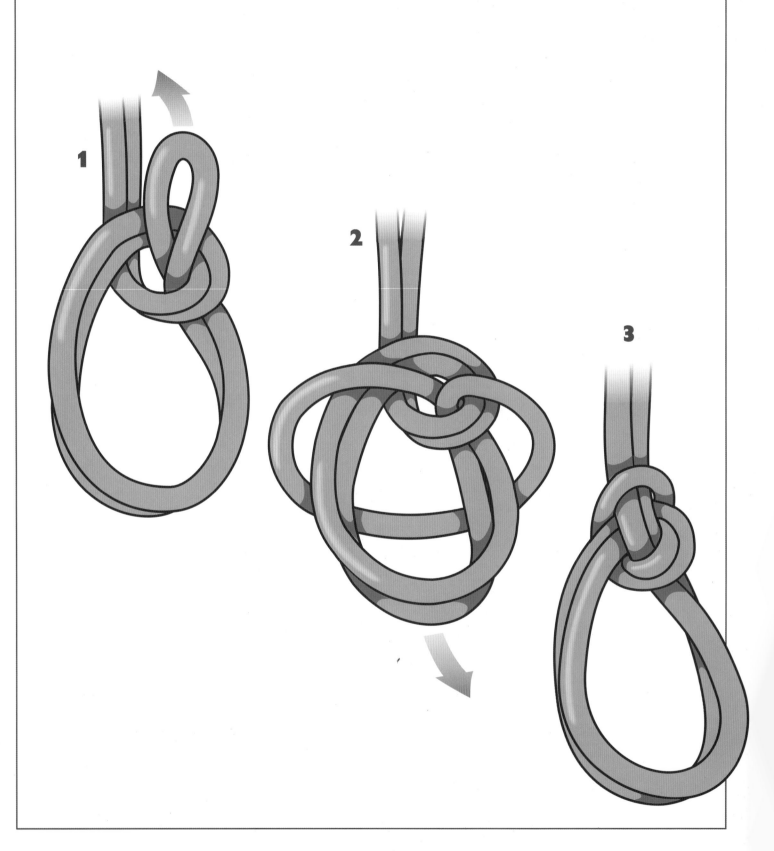

The Double Bowline

The Double Bowline is tied just like the regular Bowline except that you make an extra loop before passing the end of the rope around the standing part of the line. The result is a Double Loop Knot, which has adjustable loops—you can make one loop smaller by pulling the other loop bigger. The knot makes an excellent sling work seat. You can sit on one loop and adjust the other to fit under you arms and around your back. This leaves your hands free to carry and manipulate tools when you are aloft.

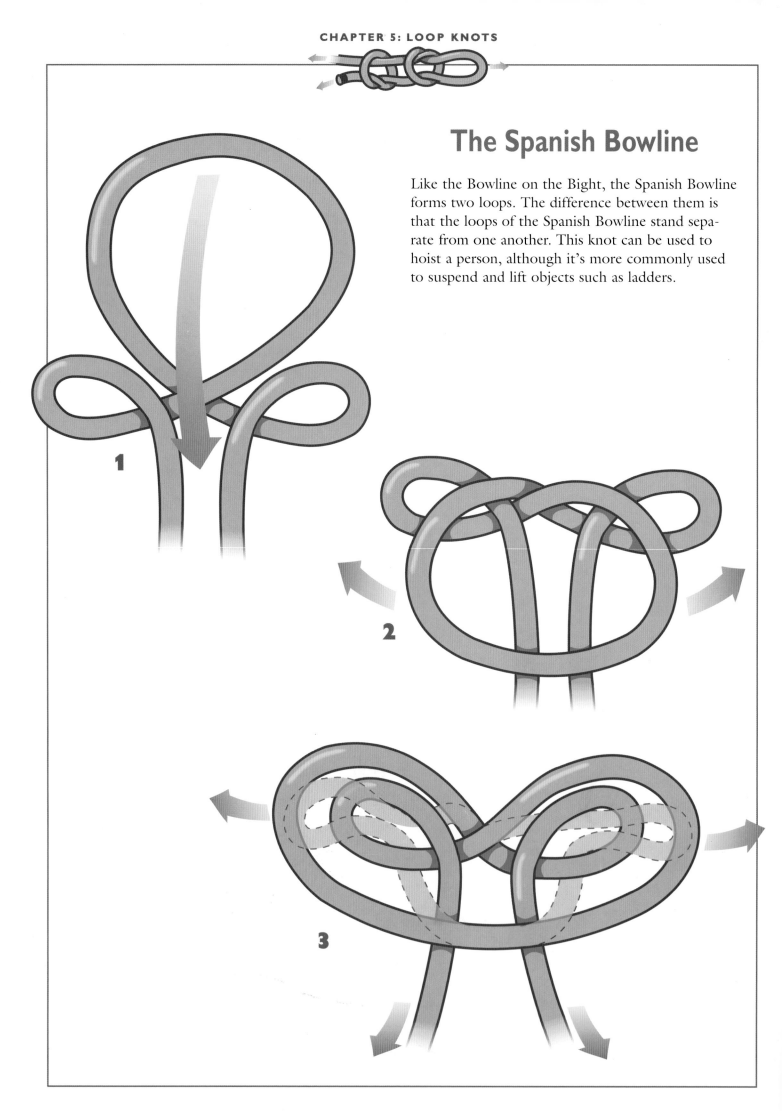

The Spanish Bowline

Like the Bowline on the Bight, the Spanish Bowline forms two loops. The difference between them is that the loops of the Spanish Bowline stand separate from one another. This knot can be used to hoist a person, although it's more commonly used to suspend and lift objects such as ladders.

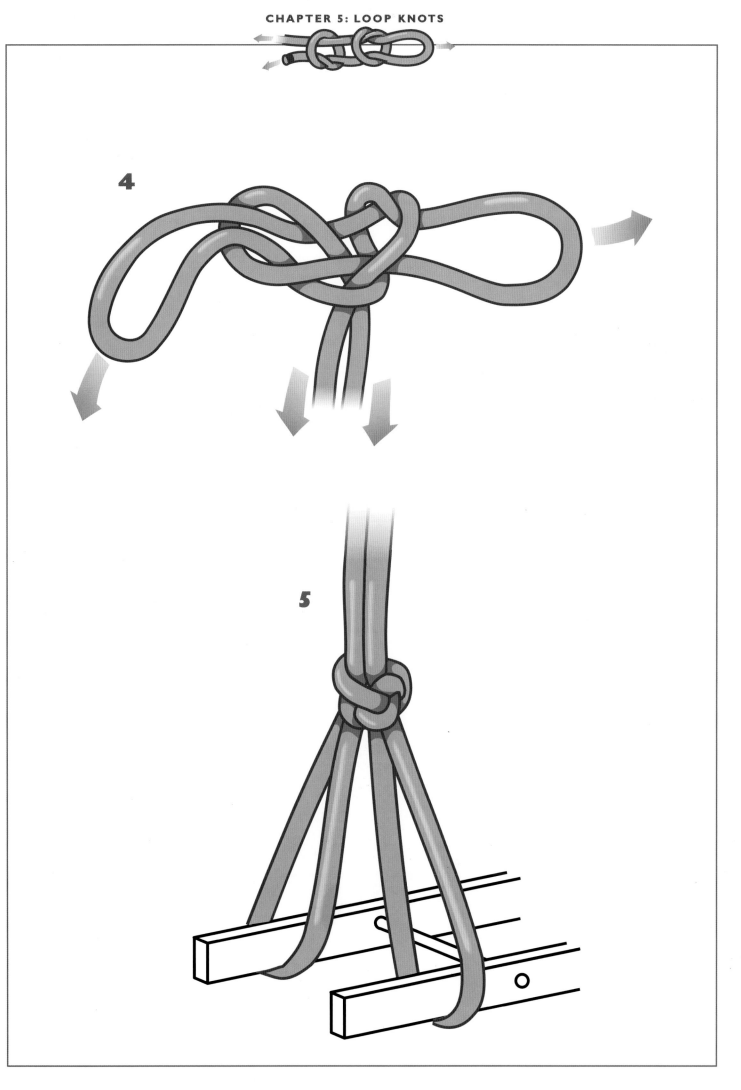

4

5

The Fisherman's Eye

The Fisherman's Eye is a fast, effective way to tie a loop in a length of fishing line. It's also appropriate for use with twine, string, or rope that's relatively small in diameter (up to about ¼-inch). It's essentially a combination of two Overhand knots that pull together to interlock. This knot is very closely related to the Fisherman's Knot (page 62).

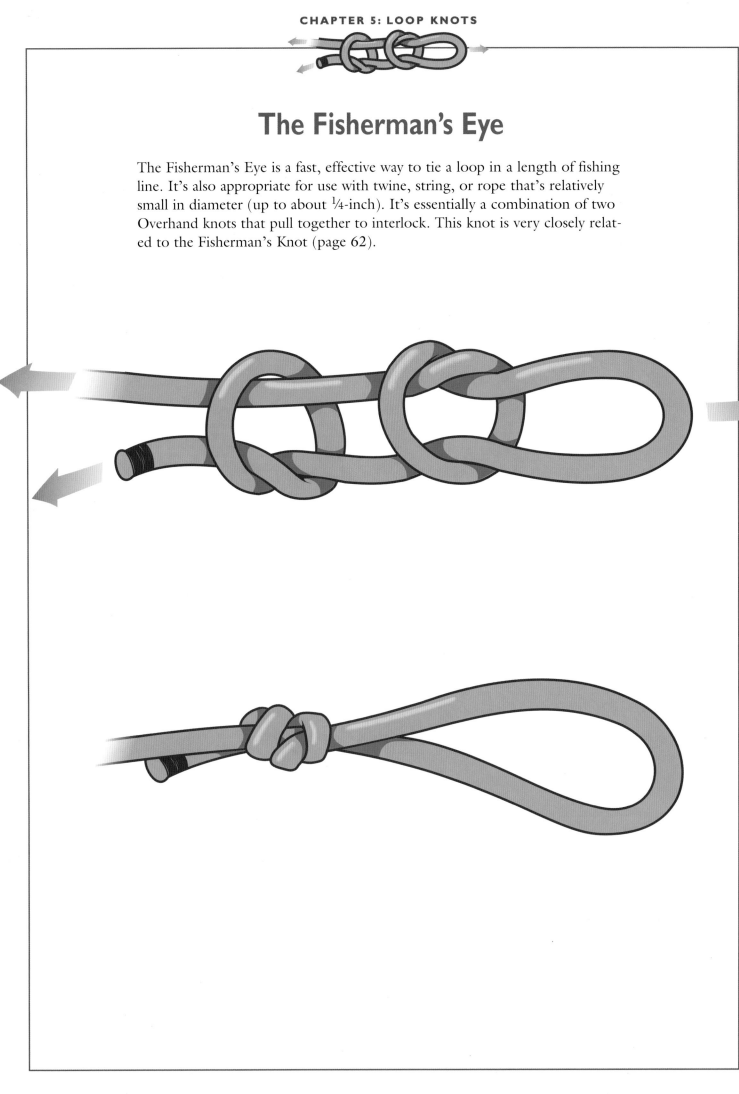

Angler's Loop

Another loop knot that's most suitable for small-diameter line (less than ⅛ inch) is the Angler's Loop. This loop is quite strong, and it won't slip. However, it does tend to jam under tension. For this reason, it's not recommended for use in large-diameter ropes.

1

2

3

Figure Eight Loop

Also known as the Flemish Eye Knot

This loop knot is essentially a Figure Eight Knot tied in the bight of a rope rather than its end. This knot is very popular with climbers for clipping on to carabiners. It's very easy to tie, quite strong, and very distinctive in appearance. This last feature makes it easy to check to make sure it's tied correctly.

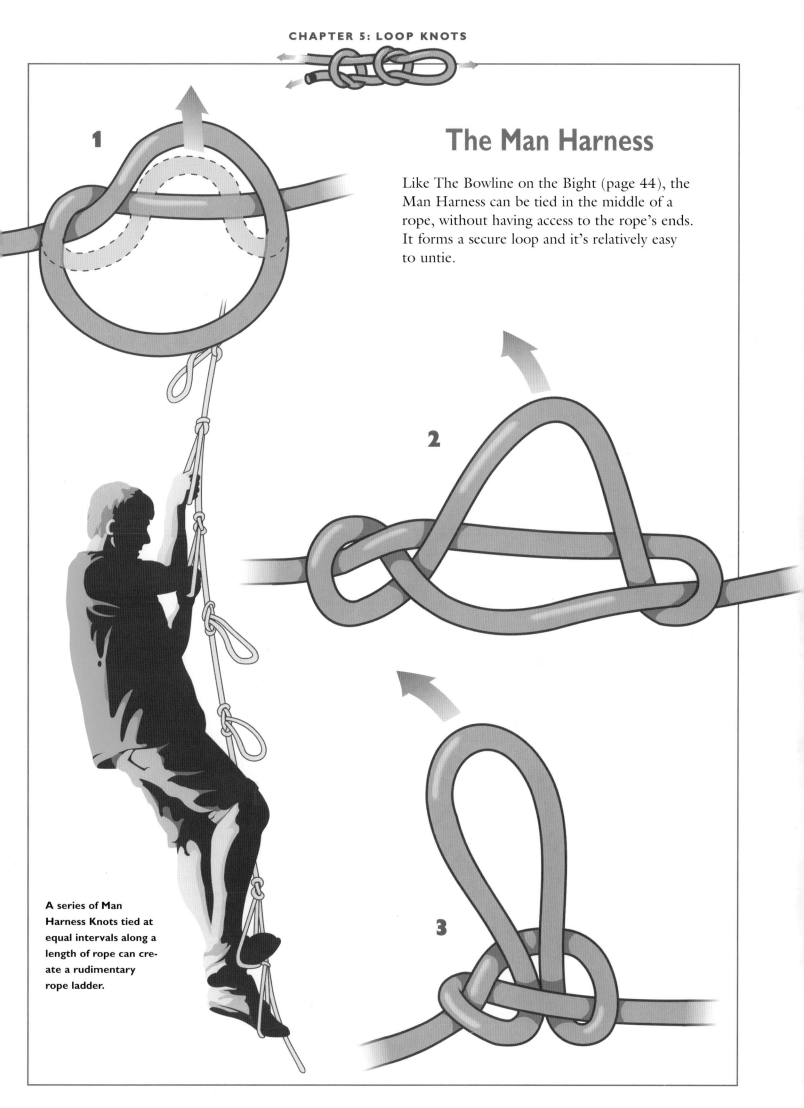

1

The Man Harness

Like The Bowline on the Bight (page 44), the Man Harness can be tied in the middle of a rope, without having access to the rope's ends. It forms a secure loop and it's relatively easy to untie.

2

3

A series of Man Harness Knots tied at equal intervals along a length of rope can create a rudimentary rope ladder.

Chapter 6
Running Knots

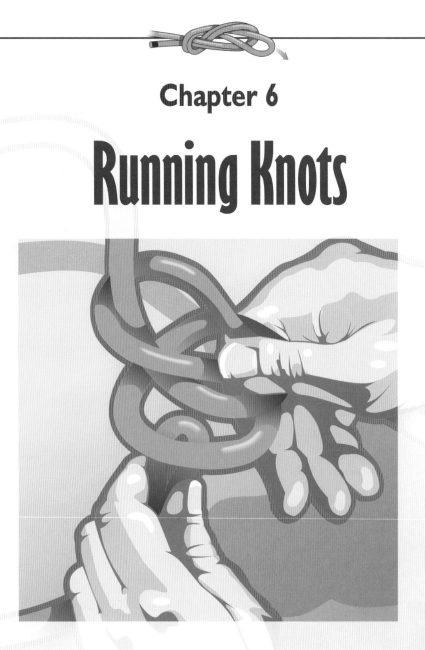

Running knots are loops that draw up tight when tension is applied. Any loop knot can be made into a running knot by pulling the standing end of the rope through the loop. The Running Bowline (page 53) is a perfect example of this. Take care NOT to tie a running loop around something that would be hurt or damaged when the loop constricts.

Running knots are useful for tying a rope to an object (such as a stray cow) that you can' t reach easily. You can either tie the knot in the rope and throw a loop around the object, or you can throw the rope over the object (assuming it's overhead) and then tie the knot in the end that's dangling down. With either method, pulling on the standing end of the rope will tighten the loop. If you need the rope back, it pays to have a plan for getting to the knot later to untie it.

The Running Bowline

The Running Bowline is made by tying a regular Bowline (page 43) with a very small loop. Pass the standing end of the rope through the loop to finish the knot. Sailors use this knot like a lariat to retrieve gear that's washed overboard.

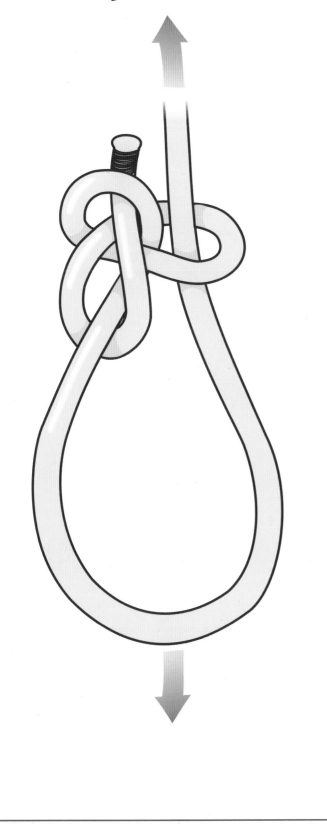

The Slip Knot

Running knots don't get much simpler than this one. The Slip Knot is essentially an Overhand Knot tied around the standing part of the rope. While it doesn't have the smooth, fast action of the Running Bowline, or of the Honda Knot (page 55), the Slip Knot does draw up tight. It's typically tied in twine used to close the top of a bag or sack.

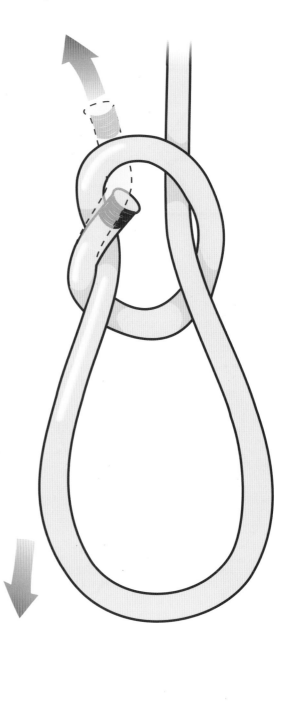

The Halter Hitch

The Halter Hitch takes the Slip Knot one step farther. Adding an extra hitch produces a knot that's easier to untie, making it a better choice for rope that you want to reuse. Don't mistake the this knot for the Neck Halter (page 30) and use it around an animal's neck to tie the animal to a post. The Halter Hitch slips and could choke the animal.

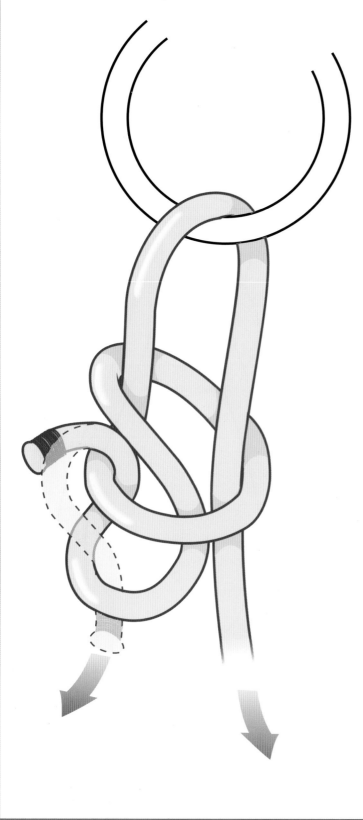

The Honda Knot

The Honda Knot, a simple running knot, is the traditional choice for tying a lariat. It's a variation of the Overhand Knot in which the working end of the rope is passed through the knot as it's drawn up. A stopper knot in the end of the rope keeps the loop from pulling out. The Matthew Walker's Knot (page 23), works nicely though a simple Overhand Knot will do. Pass the standing end of the rope through the loop to form the lariat.

1

2

3

1

2

3

4

The Hangman's Noose

What knot book would be complete without this infamous knot? While its traditional use has gone the way of the Wild West, this knot still comes in handy as decoration for the local haunted house during Halloween.

Tradition dictates you should tie the knot with thirteen turns, but in a small diameter rope, this may not look right. An acceptable noose can be tied with as few as seven turns—so use your judgment as to the appropriate proportions.

Chapter 7

Bends

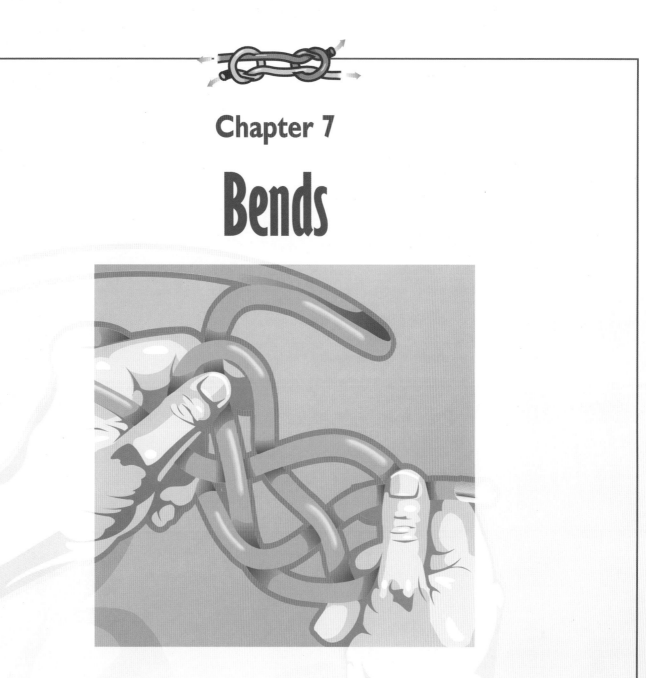

Bends are used to join the ends of two pieces of rope to make the rope longer. But because any knot tied in a rope weakens the rope, bends should be considered a temporary solution at best. If you need a longer length of rope on a permanent basis, buy the length you need rather than relying on two or more pieces tied together.

For many situations, however, a bend will be just fine, especially if the ropes being joined are of the same material and diameter.

The Sheet Bend

Also known as the Common Bend or the Flag Bend

The Sheet Bend, as its one alias suggests, is the most common bend. It ties and unties easily, and won't injure the rope's fibers. It's best tied in light- to medium-weight rope, and can be used to join ropes of different diameter together. If used for this purpose, the smaller diameter rope should pass around the larger one as shown. Keep in mind that the breaking strength of the combined rope will be less than that of the smaller line's.

Note: Compare the Sheet Bend to the Bowline (page 43) and you'll see they are essentially the same knot.

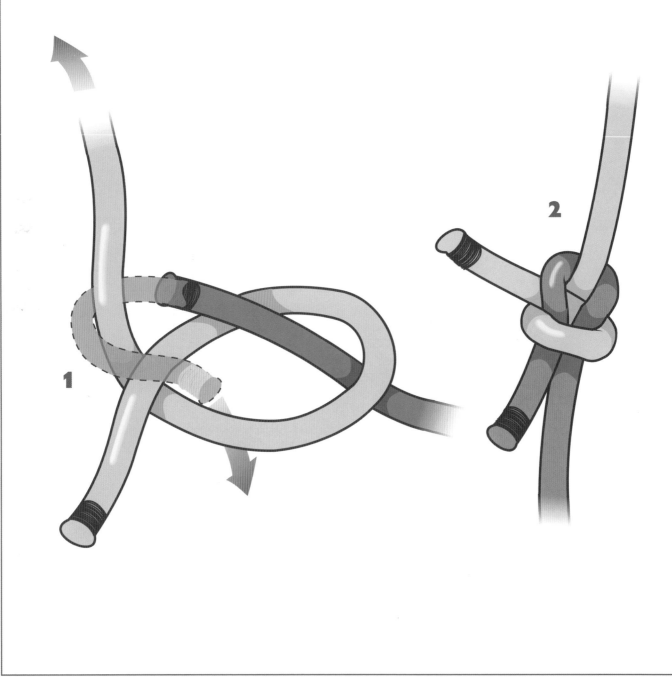

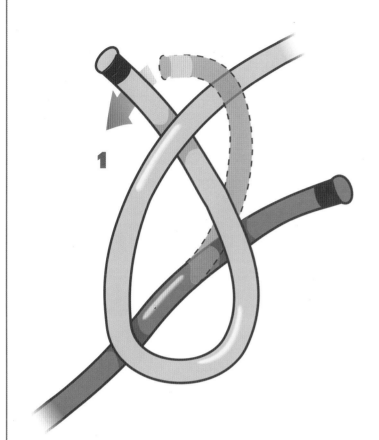

The Carrick Bend

The Carrick Bend is a very strong knot used to join heavy ropes together. It's popular among sailors and others who work with heavy lines because it always draws up correctly under load—a key consideration because knots in heavy lines often can't be tightened completely by hand. For the greatest strength and security, the ends of the lines should be seized against their respective standing parts. (See Parallel Lashing on page 77.)

When it's partially tightened, the Carrick bend forms a flat, symmetrical pattern that is quite attractive. However, as it draws up, the knot forms a bulky knob that looks nothing like the knots original, flat form. The flat look can be preserved for decorative purposes by seizing the ends before the knot is drawn up fully, but the bend won't be as strong.

Figure Eight Bend

Also known as the Flemish Bend

Because it is based on the Figure Eight Knot (page 18), this bulky bend is very easy to remember and tie. It holds securely in both rope and twine, yet is relatively easy to untie.

The Double Becket Hitch

This bend would appear to be misnamed, but originally it was, in fact, a hitch—it was used to attach a line to the becket (or eye) on the end of a whaler's harpoon. Although whaling is in decline, it seems a shame to do away with all that's associated with it—especially since this is such a sturdy knot. What are some practicle uses? In form, the Double Becket Hitch is very similar to the Sheet Bend (page 58), although the extra turn shown here makes it more secure. It too can be used to join ropes of different diameters, especially slippery synthetic ropes where the added holding power of the Double Becket Hitch comes in handy.

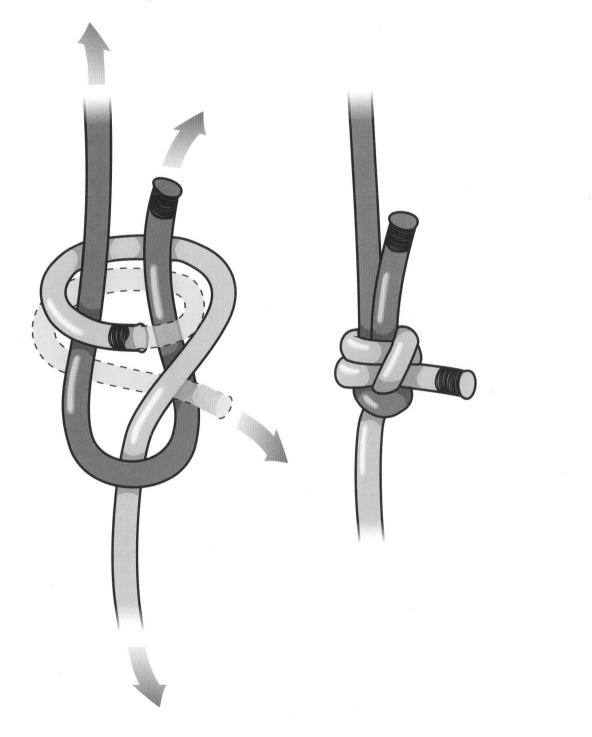

The Fisherman's Knot

Also known as the Waterman's Knot, the Halibut Knot, and the True-Lover's Bend

To join pieces of twine or string, and even small-diameter rope, it's hard to beat the Fisherman's Knot. It's widely used to tie tackle to the end of a fishing line, hence the name. But you'll find enough uses for it outside of fishing that it should be considered more than a fishing knot. It's simple to tie—really just two Overhand Knots (page 18). Plus, it comes apart readily too.

Chapter 8

Chain Knots

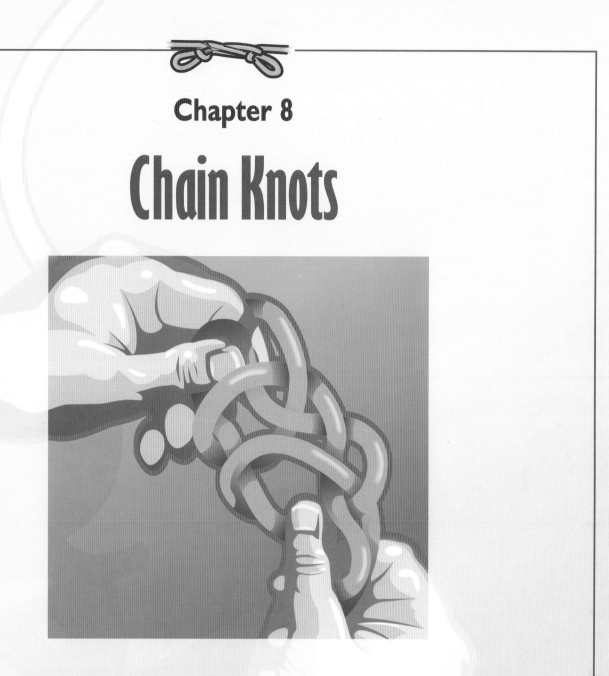

Chain knots can serve several purposes. Rather than cut a rope that is too long, a chain knot can be used to shorten it temporarily—you never know when you might need the full length. You can also tie a chain knot like the Sheepshank (page 64) to isolate a damaged section of line. Chain knots can also be used in place of coils for storing ropes and even extension cords (especially ropes and cords that are particularly stiff and don't coil well).

Sheepshank

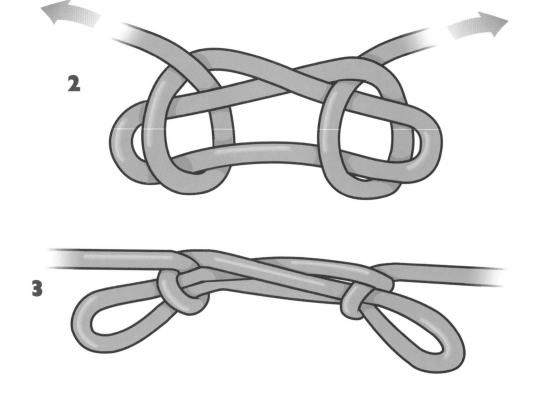

While the average Tenderfoot Scout might pale at the thought of having to tie a Sheepshank, the knot isn't especially difficult to master. It's commonly used on sail boats to take up slack in the rigging and also to shorten automobile tow ropes, as well as in other situations where you need to make a rope shorter.

A Cautionary Note: This knot holds tenaciously—as long as it's under tension. But once the line goes slack, the sheepshank will all but fall apart.

SHEEPSHANK SECRETS

The part of the rope that runs between the "ears" of the Sheepshank is under very little—if any—tension, even when the knot is fully loaded. You can take advantage of this fact in two ways: First, you can use the Sheepshank to isolate a damaged section of rope. Just make sure the damaged area ends up between the "ears."

Second, you can cut this middle section after the knot is loaded. Should you ever end up in an emergency situation where you have to leave the end of your rope tied in some inaccessible place—say at the top of a mountain—you can tie a sheep shank near the top, and cut the middle section while putting tension on the rope. Then climb down the rope. Once you're at the bottom, a quick shake will release the knot, allowing you to recover at least some of your expensive rope.

1

2

3

Chain Knot

The Chain Knot is an effective means of storing the stiffest of ropes, and even bulky extension cords. It's essentially an Overhand Loop (page 20) that is repeated until the rope is as short as you want it. For storage, the last loop can just be drawn up tight. Then a tug on the end will unravel the chain. But if you're using the knot to shorten a rope, pull the end through the last loop to lock the "chain." Then tension can be applied to the rope and the chain will hold fast.

Figure Eight Chain

The Figure Eight Chain is slightly more complicated than the Chain Knot. It makes a nice, flat strip that can be used as a belt or a carrying strap.

1

2

3

Chapter 9

Fishing Knots

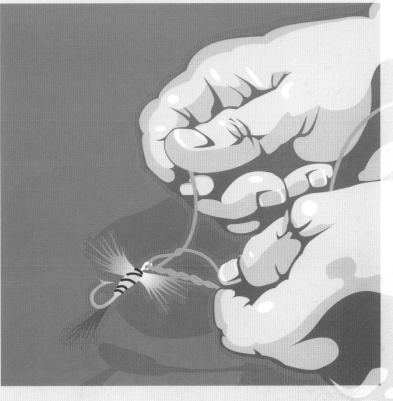

Unlike most of the other knots in this book, which can be tied in a variety of different ropes, fishing knots were developed for use with a single type of line—monofiliment fishing line. What's more, they each have a fairly specific use within the sport.

Monofiliment line presents a problem for anyone trying to knot it because it's very slippery. Most general-purpose knots will just slide apart under load. Fishing knots work better because they incorporate multiple turns and tucks, which increase the amount of bearing surface and friction within a knot.

Because monofiliment is so stiff, you may find it difficult to get a knot to draw up snugly. To resolve this, try using a drop or two of water as a lubricant to allow the knot to draw smoothly closed. You may also want to use a pair of pliers, as tugging on monofiliment with your bare hands can be painful and not particularly effective.

Note: Most fishing knots, correctly drawn up, are permanent. The only way to get them undone is to cut the line.

The Blood Knot

The Blood Knot gets its name from its resemblance to the knot that was used at the tip of a cat o' nine tails. Fortunately, within the gentle sport of angling, its use isn't as macabre. It's a good general knot for tying two lengths of mono-filiment line together. The Blood Knot is especially effective when the lines are of the same thickness.

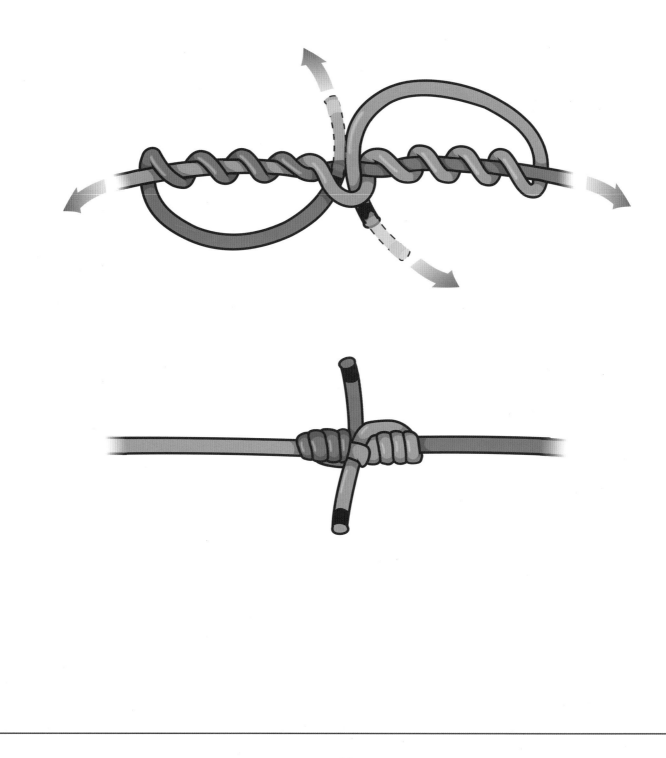

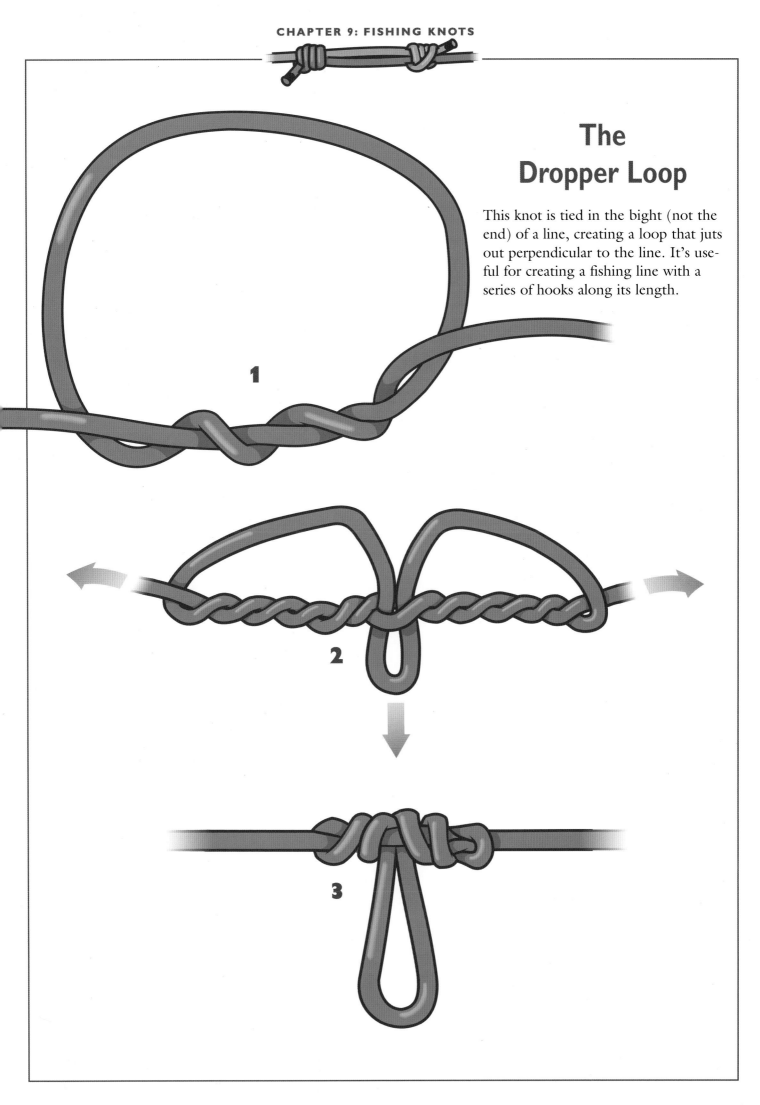

The Dropper Loop

This knot is tied in the bight (not the end) of a line, creating a loop that juts out perpendicular to the line. It's useful for creating a fishing line with a series of hooks along its length.

1

2

3

The Double Loop

The Double Knot is very similar to the Overhand Loop (page 20), although it's made with an extra turn for added security. It makes a fast, strong loop in the end of a fishing line, useful for attaching a tippet, or point.

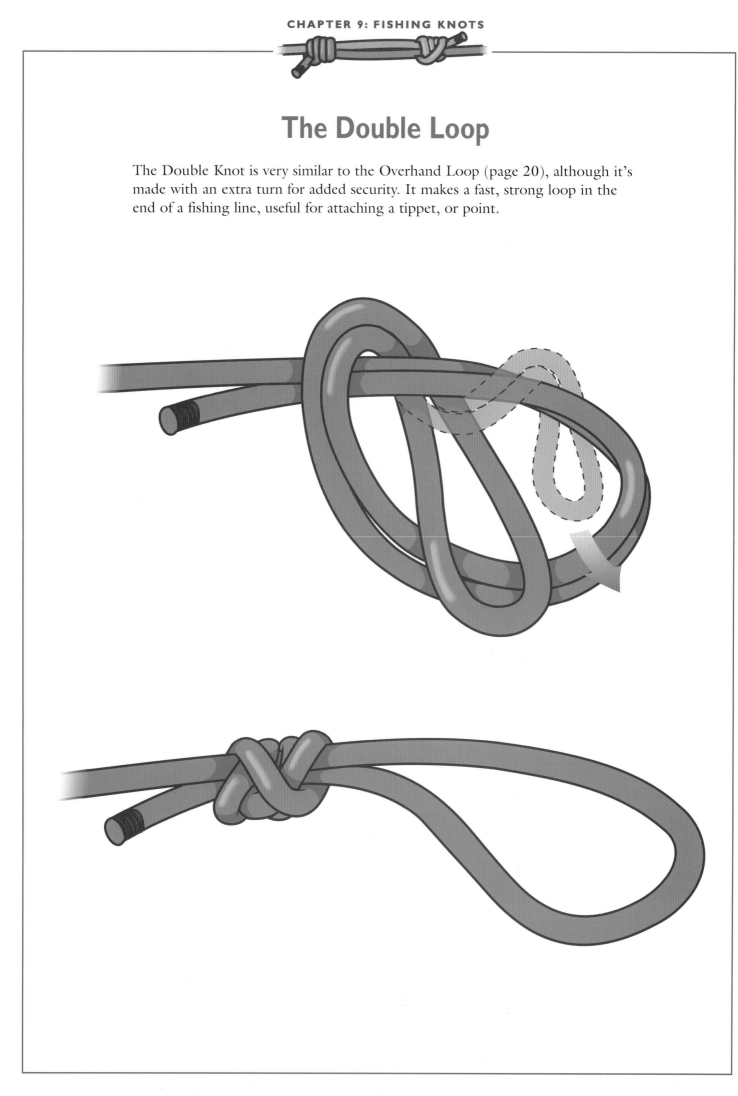

Clinch Knot

This is an easily tied knot for fastening a hook to the end of a fairly light-weight fishing line. For attaching hooks to heavier lines, the Double Loop (page 70) or the Grinner Knot (page 72) are better choices.

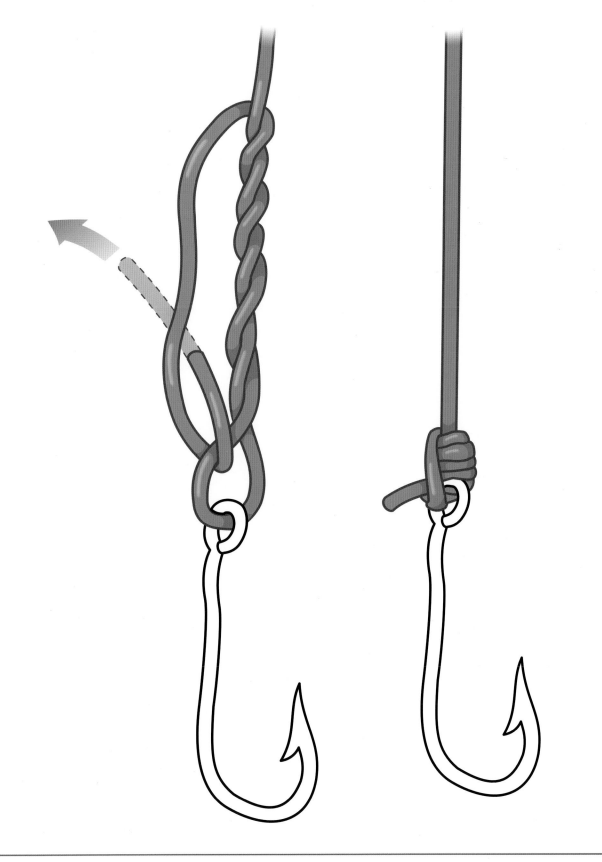

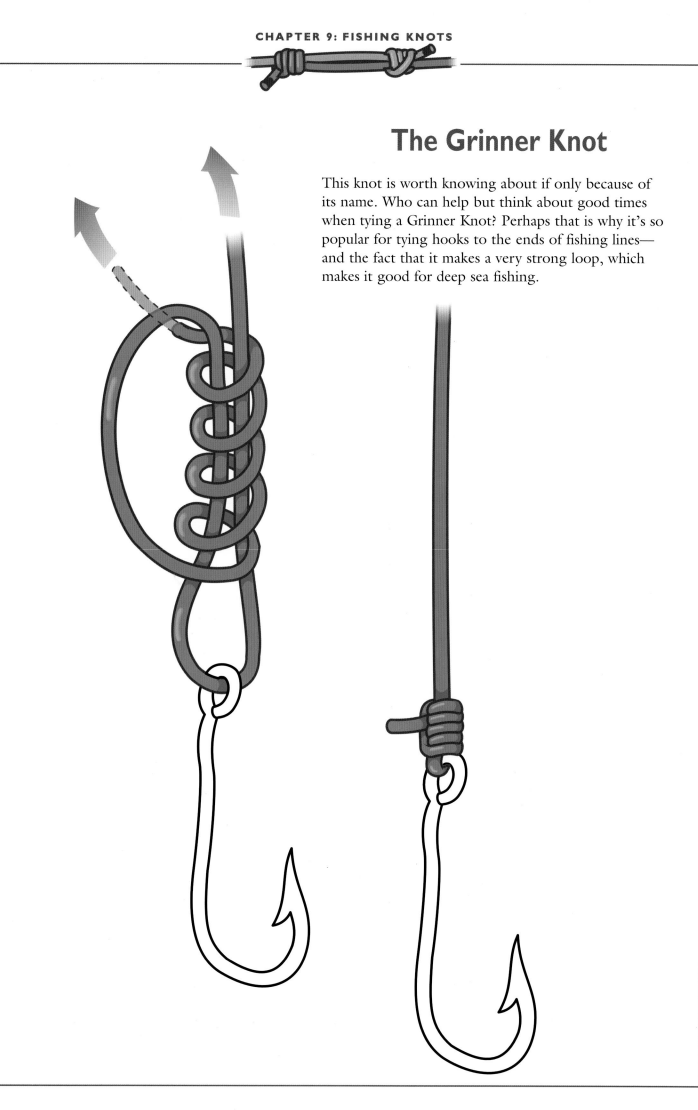

The Grinner Knot

This knot is worth knowing about if only because of its name. Who can help but think about good times when tying a Grinner Knot? Perhaps that is why it's so popular for tying hooks to the ends of fishing lines—and the fact that it makes a very strong loop, which makes it good for deep sea fishing.

The Double Grinner Knot

This knot is twice as much fun as the Grinner Knot (page 72). In fact, this knot is composed of two Grinner Knots tied to join two pieces of line together. The Double Grinner is particularly useful for joining a fine leader to the end of a casting line.

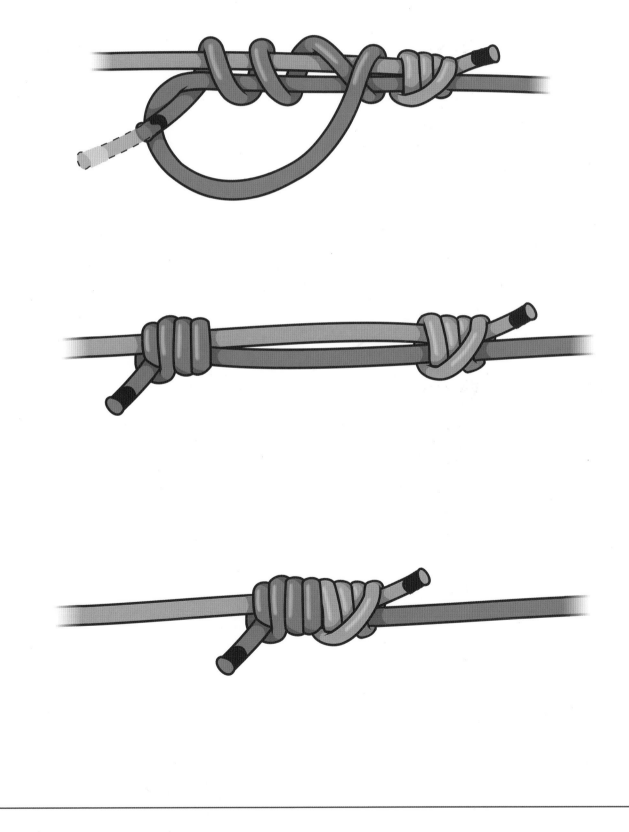

Chapter 10

Lashings

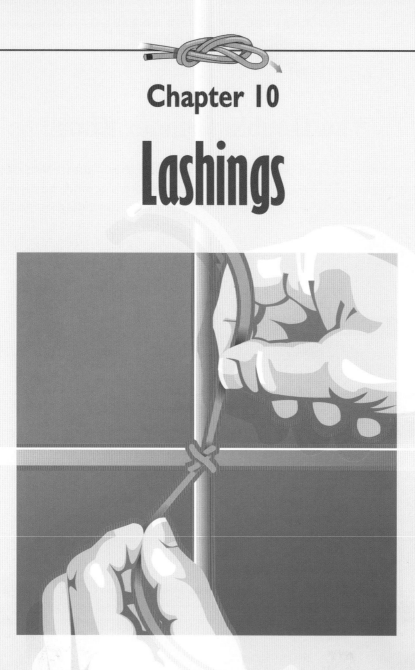

Lashings are used to bind two or more poles or sticks together. While a building inspector would probably consider a lashing a temporary connection, at best, these knots can be used to build significant structures. Visit any Boy Scout camp during the summer and you're sure to find an edifice of logs, sometimes two stories tall, lashed together.

Lashings are also handy for projects on a tamer scale. Many garden structures like trellises and arbors can be lashed together. The tied connections will probably be stronger and look better than nails or screws and can be made without any tools aside from maybe a knife.

The Transom Knot

The Transom Knot is similar to both the Clove Hitch (page 28) and the Constrictor Knot (page 41). The Transom Knot is used to join fairly small diameter poles (up to about 1 inch) together where strength isn't an issue, such as when binding the cross rails of a trellis. Depending on the size of the poles being joined, the knot should be tied with $\frac{1}{8}$-inch to $\frac{1}{4}$-inch diameter rope.

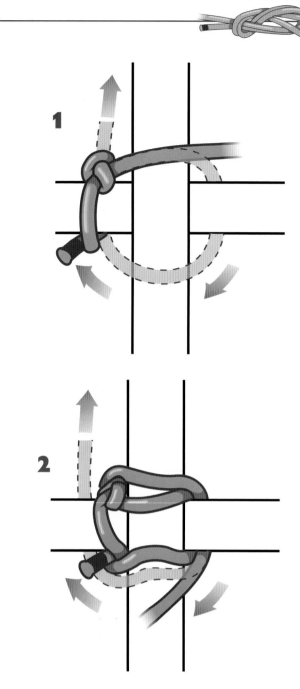

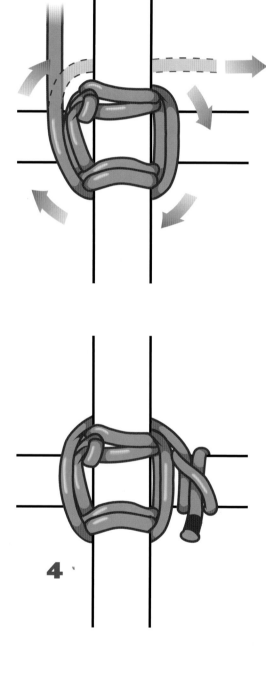

Cross Lashing

Cross Lashing is used to make a stronger right angle connection than with the Transom Knot (page 75). Cross Lashing is appropriate for joining poles 1-inch in diameter and larger. For structural applications, ½-inch diameter rope is generally appropriate.

This knot is actually a combination of knots. It starts with a Timber Hitch (page 27), which is used to join the rope to one of the poles. After wrapping the rope around the poles (three or four complete wraps is enough), the lashing is tightened with three or four frapping turns. The end of the rope is then tied off to one of the poles with a Clove Hitch (page 28).

Parallel Lashing

Parallel lashing is used to join poles side by side, either to make a longer pole, or to create an A-frame-type construction that might form the legs for a larger structure. When making an A-frame, the tops of the poles are lashed together side by side, then the bottom ends are spread to form the "A," twisting the lashing in the process.

Like the Cross Lashing on the opposite page, Parallel Lashing starts with a Timber Hitch (page 27) and the pieces are wrapped four to six times. Three or four frapping turns tighten the knot, then the end of the rope is secured with a Clove Hitch knot (page 28).

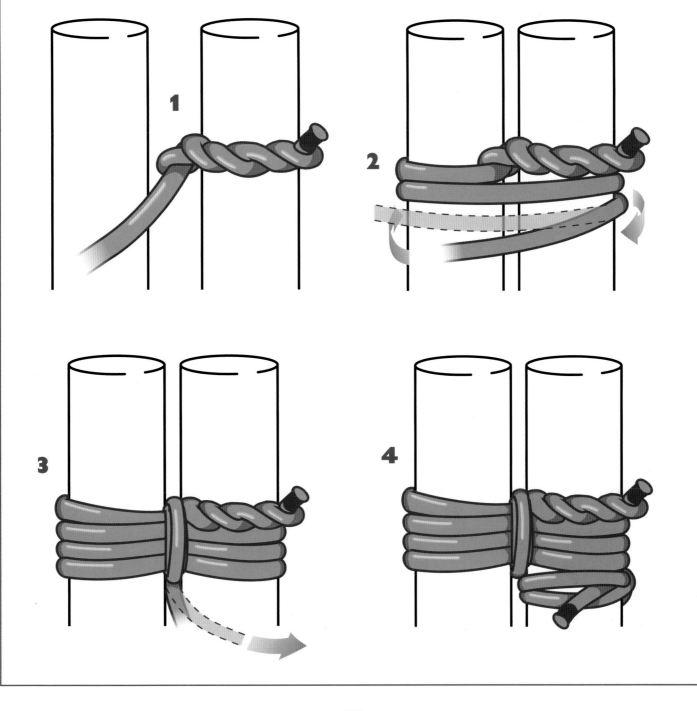

Glossary

Belay To secure a rope around a pin or other object for safety. Climbers often belay each other, with one partner taking up the slack in a safety line as the other climbs.

Bend A type of knot that's used to tie two rope together. Also, the act of tying two ropes together.

Bight The part of the rope between the two ends, especially when formed into a loop. A knot tied "in the bight" of a rope doesn't require either of the ends for completion.

Binding Knots Knots used to tie objects closed, such as packages.

Block and Tackle A set of pulleys and the rope running between them, used to move and hoist heavy objects.

Breaking Strength An estimate of the load required to cause a rope to fail.

Cable A large-diameter rope, often made of metal strands.

Capsize When a knot slips and pulls into some other (usually less secure) form it's said to have capsized.

Carabiner A metal coupling link used by rock climbers.

Chain Knots A knot or series of knots used to shorten a rope to secure it.

Cleat A wooden or metal fitting with protruding ends to which rope can be tied.

Coil To wind rope in a series of loops for storage. Also a length of rope that has been stored.

Core The inner strands of a braid rope.

Drawn Up Once tied, a knot must be "drawn up" or tightened. With many knots this process must be done slowly and carefully to insure the knot comes together correctly. An improperly drawn up knot may become a useless tangle.

Dropper A short length of fishing line used to attach a fly to the center section of the leader, between the end of the fly line and the tippet.

Fishing Knots A group of knots especially useful to anglers tying a monofiliment line.

Foul To tangle. A rope that becomes wrapped around a ship's propeller is said to have "fouled the prop."

Frapping Turns Turns of rope taken around a lashing to draw the parts together.

Fray To unravel. Cut ropes will often fray at the ends unless the ends are whipped, or secured with a stopper knot.

Hard Knot Any knot that jams and becomes difficult to untie.

Hard Laid Rope with strands that are tightly twisted together. Hard laid ropes are usually fairly stiff.

Hawser A large rope, usually 5 to 24 inches in diameter, often used for towing or mooring.

Hawser Laid Ordinary, three strand rope is said to be "hawser laid."

Hitch A knot that ties a rope to another object such as a ring or pole.

Jam A knot that's difficult to untie or draw up. Many knots that undo easily when dry will jam when wet.

Laid Line A rope made from strands that are twisted, not braided together.

Lashing   A means of binding poles with rope.

Lay   The direction the strands of a rope are twisted. Most laid ropes are right-laid—the strands spiral up to the right when the rope is viewed vertically.

Leader   A length of monofiliment fishing line that runs between the end of the fly line and the fly.

Line   A generic term for a rope that has no specific purpose.

Loop Knots   Knots that form a loop in a line.

Make Fast   To secure a rope with a hitch or other knot.

Noose   Any of a number of loop knots that draw up tight under load.

Plait   To braid several strands together, also the resulting braid.

Rigging   In the broadest sense, all the rope on a ship. The running rigging is secured at one end only, the standing rigging is secured at both ends.

Round Turn   To loop a rope around an object twice.

Running Knots   Knots that form loops which constrict under load.

S-Laid   Rope that is laid up with a left-handed twist. Not very common.

Safe Working Load (SWL)   An estimate of the amount of load a rope can safely support given its age, condition, and the knots being used.

Sailor's Knot   A generic term for any unfamiliar or well-tied knot.

Seizing   A connection made by lashing one rope to another or to itself. Knots can be made more secure by seizing the working ends back against the standing part of the rope.

Small Stuff   Rope, string, cord, or twine under ½ inch in diameter.

Soft Laid   Rope with strands that are loosely twisted together. Soft laid rope is generally fairly limp.

Standing End or Part   The end of the rope away from the end that is being knotted.

Stopper Knot   A knot used to keep the end of a rope from pulling through a hole, grommet, or pulley. Stopper knots also can be used to keep the end of a rope from unraveling.

Strand   A bundle of fibers or yarns twisted together to form a single piece. Most rope is made up of three strands.

Tag End   The end of a fly fishing line to which the leader is attached—also known as the working end.

Tether   To tie an animal or object to keep it from getting away.

Thimble   A metal eye around which a loop is tied (often in steel cable). The thimble maintains the shape of the loop and prevents wear.

Throwing Coil   A way of wrapping rope that increases the weight at the rope's end, which is useful for throwing the rope a far distance.

Tippet (or point)   The end of the leader to which a fly is attached.

Turn   To loop a rope around an object or another rope.

Whip   To bind the end of a rope to keep it from fraying.

Working End   The end of the rope that is being knotted—also known as the tag end.

Yarn   Individual fibers are spun into yarns, which in turn are spun into strands, which are twisted to form rope.

Z-Laid   Rope laid up with a right-handed twist.

About the Author

Ken Burton is a woodworker and a writer living outside of New Tripoli, Pennsylvania. His other books include *Jigs, Fixtures, and Setups* (Rodale Press 1992) and *The Weekend Woodworker Annual* (Rodale Press 1994). An avid camper, he first learned about knots and ropework while earning the rank of Eagle Scout.

Burton is currently putting the finishing touches on his woodshop, which he built from strawbales.

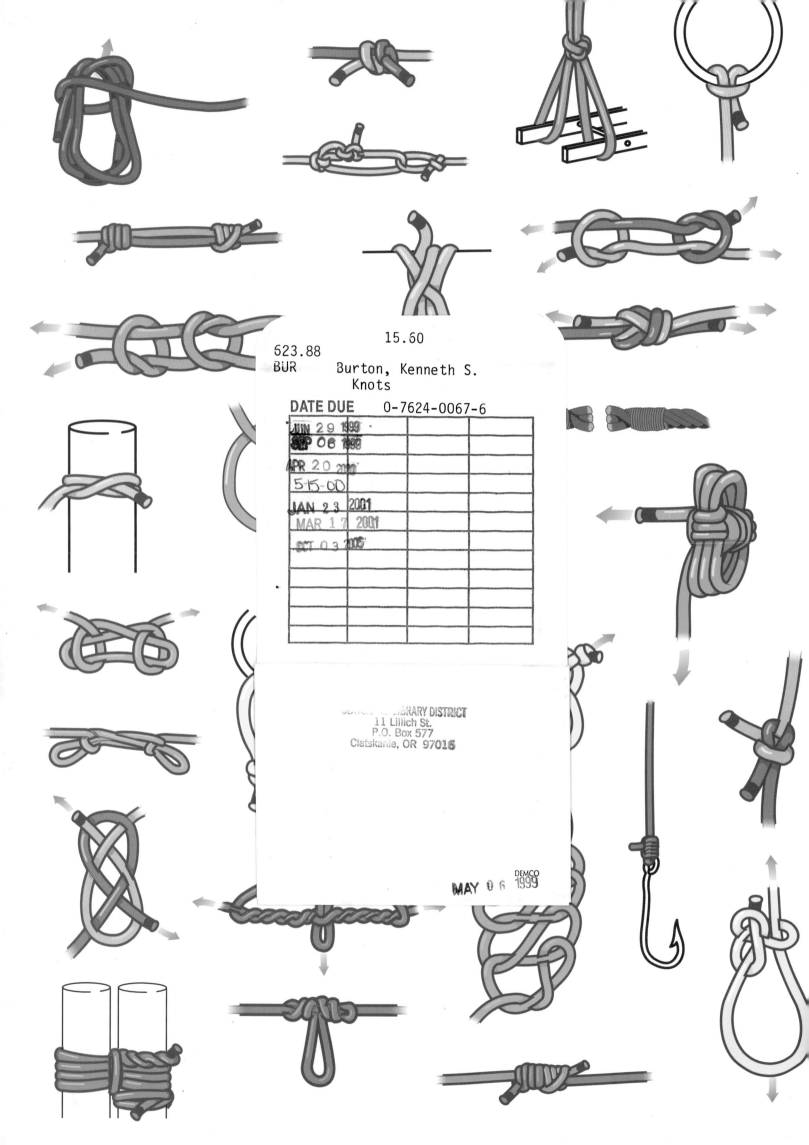